THE SCREENWRITER'S HANDBOOK

THE SCREENWRITER'S HANDBOOK

What to Write, How to Write It, Where to Sell It

CONSTANCE NASH
and
VIRGINIA OAKEY

PERENNIAL LIBRARY

Harper & Row, Publishers
New York, Cambridge, Philadelphia, San Francisco
London, Mexico City, São Paulo, Singapore, Sydney

THE SCREENWRITER'S HANDBOOK. Copyright © 1978 by Constance Nash and Virginia Oakey. All rights reserved. Printed in the United States of America. No part of this book may be used or reproduced in any manner without written permission except in the case of brief quotations embodied in critical articles and reviews. For information address Harper & Row, Publishers, Inc., 10 East 53d Street, New York, N. Y. 10022. Published simultaneously in Canada by Fitzhenry & Whiteside Limited, Toronto.

Designed by Eve Callahan

FIRST EDITION

LIBRARY OF CONGRESS CATALOG CARD NUMBER: 77–76031

ISBN: 0–06–013162–4

ISBN: 0–06–463454–X (PBK)

86 87 88 89 90   20 19 18 17 16 15 14 13 12 11

Contents

Acknowledgments   vii

Preface   ix

1. THE ESSENTIAL ELEMENTS   1

   How to Plan Your Screenplay   1
   Characterization   4
   Dialog   7
   Style   15

2. HOW TO WRITE THE SCREENPLAY   18

   Organization   18
   Three Acts   20
   Screenplay Styles   22
   Terminology   27
   Rough Draft   37
   Rewriting   41

3. SCRIPT FORMAT   43

    Script Title Page   43
    Typewriter Settings   44
    Title Page for Treatments or Outlines   46
    Variations for Television Formats   47
    Number of Scripts Needed   48

4. INTERVIEWS   50

    Ernest Lehman, screenwriter-producer-director   51
    Robert Evans, producer   58
    Delbert Mann, director-producer   64
    Frank Rosenfelt, President, Metro-Goldwyn-Mayer   71
    Michael Zimring, literary agent   75
    Gene Wilder, actor-director-screenwriter   80

5. PRACTICAL BUSINESS ADVICE   85

    How to Market Your Screenwriting Talent   85
    How to Get an Agent   86
    "Spec" Scripts   88
    Copyrights, Contracts, Options   89
    Writers Guild of America, West   90
    Writers' Representatives   103
    Schools and Publications   110
    Interview—Eric Weissmann, attorney-at-law   113

6. EXCERPTS FROM SCREENPLAYS AND
    TREATMENT   122

    Excerpt, *Chinatown* by Robert Towne   122
    Excerpt, *The Sound of Music* by Ernest Lehman   128
    Excerpt, *The Adventures of Sherlock Holmes'*
       Smarter Brother by Gene Wilder   137
    Excerpt, *Game of Pawns* by William MacAllister   139
    Excerpt, Treatment for *Katie's Ladies* by Constance
       Nash   142

    Index   146

Acknowledgments

—Our warmest thanks to Isabelle Ziegler, writer-editor-teacher, Douglas Laurence, producer, and Eric Weissmann, our legal mentor, whose professional advice and constant encouragement sustained us, from Preface to Index.

—Our gratitude to all of our interviewees who so generously made time for us in their incredibly busy schedules: Robert Evans, Ernest Lehman, Delbert Mann, Frank Rosenfelt, Eric Weissmann, Gene Wilder, and Michael Zimring.

—Our appreciation to Robert Towne and Ernest Lehman for their permission to use excerpts from their Academy Award–winning screenplays, and to Gene Wilder and William MacAllister for the use of excerpts from their screenplays.

—Our appreciation for invaluable assistance received from Eduardo Guerini, legal counsel for Paramount Pictures Corporation, Michael H. Franklin, executive director, Writers Guild of America, West, the American Film Institute, Sherwood Oaks Experimental College, and Writers Guild of America, West, Inc.

Preface

As a viewer you already know that films are an audio-visual art form. As a writer you should also know that, first of all, they must evoke a strong emotional response. The audience has to react viscerally to the plight of your characters whether they are larger-than-life heroes and villains or seagulls and dolphins. What the audience sees and hears does not stand alone. Behind the sights and sounds, and enlarged through them, is the spirit of *you*, the screenwriter, as it is sifted through your imagination, your experience, and your view of the world about which you write.

As a screenwriter you should keep constantly in mind that your audience must become emotionally rather than intellectually engrossed in what is unreeling on the screen. Television programs have commercial breaks; plays have intermissions; and one can always put a book down. But in a movie theater the audience has no time for introspection, for pondering, or for questioning the film's intent. The film reels steadily onward and the audience must know, or believe it knows, what is happening every second. This does not mean that there will be no dramatic surprises; it means simply that there must be no surprises which do not, as they unfold, make total sense to the audience. Loose ends or unexplained developments will cause a loss of audience concentration and strike a heavy blow against your screenplay's success.

As you write, put yourself in the audience. Try to see through its eyes and to anticipate its expectations and reactions. Continually reach out to it; do not expect it to reach out to you unless you have made it imperative for it to do so. You have to go the whole way.

Motion pictures are just that—pictures that move, giving the illusion of actual events on the screen before you. It is through this process that your creation will, in a magic sense, achieve reality. Whether you enlarge the vision of your audience or shake its complacency or plague its dreams is up to you. It is essential to the success of your screenplay that your audience is made to *experience* it.

The Essential Elements

All creative writing begins with an idea. How the screenplay idea came to you, the exact moment of inspiration, may forever elude you. But its insistence on being born, on becoming black-on-white, then transferred in glorious color to a wide screen in a darkened theater is something that will not elude you. You have to write it.

So, first there is the compelling idea. Whether it springs from a character, a situation, an experience, or a philosophical persuasion, it can be churned through the mill of creative expression only through concentrated and disciplined effort.

After the initial concept has taken hold, you will be concerned about the plot, the characterizations, and the dialog. These are the basic ingredients of any screenplay, and your mastery of them will require total dedication.

HOW TO PLAN YOUR SCREENPLAY

Choose your stance: Will your screenplay derive its major strength through (1) its characters, (2) its theme, or (3) its situation? Any substantial screenplay will contain all three, but, depending upon your unique vision, the stress will be on one of them.

One Flew Over the Cuckoo's Nest, despite its strong theme (a free spirit in rebellion against the Establishment), is primarily concerned with the character of the protagonist. *Sounder* is an example of a thematic script, with its theme of man's resistance to incredible misery. *The Towering Inferno* and similar disaster films in which total catastrophe seems inevitable are more concerned with the situation and ensuing action.

Whatever your stance, hold tightly to your original idea so that your script will maintain balance and integrity of purpose. If you change directions midway, your screenplay will become unwieldy and lose focus.

CONFLICT AND CRISES

There is no drama without conflict. Nearly all stories are told through a problem or problems which your characters must meet and overcome, or be overcome by. Your plot will be developed through these problems, how or why they occur, and how they are resolved. The most traumatic moments for your characters are the crises (or plot points) around which your screenplay will be constructed.

CLIMAX

Know exactly where you are going with your script. Know the climax—which is arrived at when all the problems are resolved. All things lead to it, and you should keep that in mind from the first word you write. It is your destination and once you lose sight of it, the power of your script becomes diffused and disoriented. Eventually you may decide to change the ending, but it must be your reasoned choice, not something foisted upon you because your plot got out of control.

SCRIPT DIVISIONS

Divide your script into several parts or acts, preferably three. Determine what you mean to say in each, how each will be developed, and how each will build to a crisis that will propel the story forward. The acts will provide the framework within which your

script will be filled out, and will serve as your guide in writing the
rough draft (see chapter 2). The following diagram illustrates this:

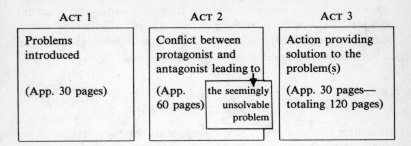

ACT 1	ACT 2	ACT 3
Problems introduced (App. 30 pages)	Conflict between protagonist and antagonist leading to (App. 60 pages) the seemingly unsolvable problem	Action providing solution to the problem(s) (App. 30 pages— totaling 120 pages)

Keep in mind that all the action leads into and away from the time
of the seemingly unsolvable problem. A screenplay is a series of
crises; the first comes at the beginning, within the first few pages, to
make a change of status quo in the protagonist's situation. Each
crisis will be more severe than the last, finally rising to the climax
which comes at or toward the end of act 3.

An example of a writer's skillful handling of a crisis leading to a
climax occurs with the last speech of the play *Marty* by Paddy
Chayefsky. The audience does not know, even at this late moment,
what Marty plans to do about his association with the "dog" of a
girl who is scorned by his family and his friend.

> MARTY
> You don't like her. My mother don't
> like her. She's a dog, and I'm a fat,
> ugly little man. All I know is I had
> a good time last night. I'm gonna have
> a good time tonight. If we have enough
> good times together, I'm going down on
> my knees and beg that girl to marry me.
> If we make a party again this New Year's,
> I gotta date for the party. You don't
> like her, that's too bad.

TREATMENT

If you have written a treatment of your screenplay (a 15–45-page résumé of it) you can work directly from it. It will be an excellent guide to keep you from straying off the path that will lead inevitably, but never predictably, to your predetermined climax. (See chapter 2 for details. Also, see excerpt from a treatment in chapter 6.)

CHARACTERIZATION

A film play is about human beings who, for the duration of the film, are worth caring about. They are real, they are interesting, and they engage the audience's attention. No matter what the audience feels for them—admiration or contempt or affection—the characters must elicit strong emotional reactions. We are speaking, of course, of the principal characters and the important supporting players.

Get to know your principals. Don't merely become acquainted with them. Make notes on everything you know about them as if you were a psychologist (and good writers are fairly good psychologists). Know their occupations, motivations, habits, fears, prejudices, vices, pleasures, how they walk and dress and talk. Know them as you know yourself.

Build the conflict between the protagonist and the antagonist, making the villain an opponent worthy of the hero. At the climax the audience must be made to feel that they have fought their best fight, regardless of who the victor is.

STEREOTYPES

Avoid stereotyped characters. This is the timid or lazy writer's approach. The mousy librarian, the absent-minded professor, the mindless macho truck driver, the whore-with-a-heart-of-gold have been written about so often that they may seem safe to the beginning screenwriter. Stop thinking about them in this hackneyed context. Each is a unique human being; portray her/him as such. (The mousy schoolteacher may yearn to be a belly dancer and practice arduously in the privacy of her apartment.)

MOTIVATION

Motivation means the *reason* for a character's behavior. Your plot construction demands that your protagonist must endure severe philosophical or emotional changes. For them he must be strongly motivated—given reasons which the audience understands. (A brave man can perform a cowardly act, but his reasons must be made clear either prior to or after the fact.)

CONSISTENCY

A human being has no discernible character until he acts. In films, of course, dialog is a form of action. So the people you depict must reveal their inner selves through what they say and do; speech and action must be consistent with the character you have given them.

It is quite possible for a basically honest and good man to commit a felony—and for it to be consistent with his character. A splendid example of this occurs in the film *Sounder.* (screenplay by Lonne Elder III). It was consistent with Nathan Lee's character, though he was an honorable man, to steal meat from a white neighbor's smokehouse. Already established, along with his basic goodness, was his deep and abiding love for his wife and children and his agony at being unable to keep them adequately fed. In fact, the audience is made to wonder how such a man could have done anything else. It was not an intelligent act, since he risked a sentence at the work farm, but it was a very human act, committed out of love, in the passion of despair. And it was not at all inconsistent with his character.

CONTRASTS

The dramatic interplay between characters depends heavily upon contrasts. Your characters, even within a single family unit, must have obvious differences, both physical and psychological. Your protagonist and antagonist need not be poles apart. For example, both can be oil riggers or advertising executives. But individually they must be molded from very different clay. It will be these differences that will spark the conflict from which your crises will arise. Remember that your antagonist need not be another human being.

It can be the weather—a tornado, flood, or drought; or an oppressive society, a despotic political regime, etc.

ENVIRONMENT

If you are not familiar with the environment in which you have placed your characters, research it carefully. No human being is totally molded by his environment, yet none remains untouched by it. If, for instance, you have chosen the Louisiana bayou country for your setting, you will have to know what particular effect this particular place has on its inhabitants.

Time is part of environment, too, whether it is the later 1970s or the 1890s. Any period earlier than the last decade should be researched for customs, social mores and behavior, modes of dress, and so on. Be at home in the environment, because until the completion of your screenplay your life will be spent there—at least during your working hours.

CHARACTER EXPOSITION

Fully explain your characters through dialog, behavior, and appearance. Never allow the audience to wonder (except when such uncertainty is needed for plot development) just what manner of man/woman a character really is.

You must know how your characters talk, their vocabularies, idioms, slang, and habitual use of certain expressions. They must reveal themselves through the *way* they speak (what makes them yell, whisper, or whine? Or become mute, which is another revelatory device).

Their behavior will be dictated by the inner lives you have given them. Whether they are violent or passive, brutal or compassionate, they are your creations. Expose them through their actions as well as their speech.

Appearances should be revealing, too. If it is a costume film, the costumes must be painstakingly researched. Clothes in contemporary America are also costumes. A small-town attorney does not dress like a beach bum. A Midwest farmer does not dress like a Los Angeles swinger.

MINOR CHARACTERS

It is impossible, unless the cast is very small, to fully develop minor characters. The best way to distinguish them is by giving each a single differentiating trait or characteristic which will make him interesting.

Remember this about your characters: if the audience is allowed to feel ho-hum about them, whether hero or villain, you have failed your screenplay.

DIALOG

Your ear for dialog is extremely important to the success of your screenplay. Your characters will reveal themselves not only through what they say but the way they say it.

Every word of dialog must count for something: (1) to suggest the theme, (2) set the tone, (3) reveal the characters, (4) present an immediate problem, and (5) advance the plot.

An example of dialog that *suggests the theme* and also *sets the tone* occurs within the first ten minutes (ten pages) of *The Godfather* (screenplay by Mario Puzo and Francis Ford Coppola). Don Corleone, the godfather, is in the library, and his henchman, Hagen, has handed him a list of names of persons who are waiting to see him. (At this point in the screenplay Don Corleone has spoken only six words.)

                    DON CORLEONE
          What will these people ask of me?

                       HAGEN
          Anthony Coppola. He needs money to
          open a restaurant. He'll ask for
          five hundred dollars.

Don Corleone waits questioningly.

                       HAGEN
          His father worked with you when you
          were young.

The godfather smiles. A good memory.

                    HAGEN
               (continuing)
          Francesco Hippi. His nephew has been
          refused parole. A bad case. But
          he hopes you can do something or else
          the boy serves another five years.

The Don is impassive on this one.

                    HAGEN
          Amerigo Bonasera. The two boys who
          beat up his daughter and tried rape
          got off with suspended sentences.
          He wants revenge.

The godfather turns away.

                    HAGEN
          Johnny Fontane. Your godson is in
          trouble again. There's a big part
          in a new movie he wants. But the
          studio boss won't give it to him.

                    DON CORLEONE
          Why not?

Hagen shrugs.

                    HAGEN
          Then there's Luca Brasi. I don't
          know what he wants. And a few others,
          very minor.

                    DON CORLEONE
          Leave Bonasera to the last.

Though the godfather speaks very few words, this dialog clearly defines his all-powerful position among the Italian families in his community. He is their king, and they come to him seeking his favor and his favors. The theme is suggested and the tone is set.

An example of dialog that *reveals the character* is the following excerpt from *Maggie Walker* (screenplay by Isabelle Ziegler and

Virginia Oakey). Elizabeth Walker, mother of the child protagonist, Maggie, is convinced that Maggie should not attempt to go to school, believing that a black girl in the South of the 1870s is not entitled to such an exalted ambition. In this scene, Elizabeth walks along the street one evening and is stopped by an adolescent girl, Bitsy, who asks her to come in and look at her sick baby. After Elizabeth tends to the baby, she looks closely at his adolescent mother.

                    ELIZABETH
        Bitsy! You in the family way again?

                    BITSY
        Yes'm, I reckon I is.

                    ELIZABETH
        You got more than you can handle right
        now with Bubba. You don't need no more
        babies.

                    BITSY
        No'm, I didn't never count on having
        Bubba . . . and now I got me another one on
        the way. With just me and Mama, and no
        man in the house, it's real hard. I
        sure wish I could see an end to it.

                    ELIZABETH
        I wish you could, too, child. You too
        young for the hard life that's been
        put on you.

INT. - MAGGIE'S CABIN

                    ELIZABETH
        I always say that you're quick and you're
        strong and that oughta be enough for you.
        But the good Lord give you brains and we
        ain't gonna commit the mortal sin of
        wasting 'em. Next month you gonna start
        to that school.

This dialog reveals Elizabeth as an intelligent though uneducated woman who is both compassionate and imaginative. She can see in Bitsy's plight what could happen to her own daughter and does not hesitate to make a decision which to her (a former slave) is a tremendously courageous one. The dialog with Bitsy not only reveals Elizabeth's character but provides impetus for a change in her attitude.

An example of dialog that *presents an immediate problem* is found in the opening scene of *Sounder.*

The film opens with the father, Nathan Lee Morgan, and his son, David Lee, hunting possums on a clear cold autumn night, accompanied by their hound, Sounder.

The first dialog in the screenplay:

> DAVID LEE
> There ain't no possums in this woods
> tonight, Daddy.

> NATHAN LEE
> Looks that way, son. Guess the cold
> done drove most of 'em down to the
> big water country - but if there's one
> left out there - we gotta find him.

> DAVID LEE
> It's cold, Daddy!

> NATHAN LEE
> Here, put my jacket over you.

From this brief exchange we know that it is extremely important for Nathan Lee to find and kill a possum: "we gotta find him." His son is cold, the hunt has been frustrating, yet he persists. Why? The immediate problem is obvious: they need food for their table.

Continuing with *Sounder,* there is an excellent example of dialog used to *advance the plot* in the scene following Nathan Lee's return to his cabin after the fruitless possum hunt. His wife, Rebecca, discovers that David Lee has eaten some walnuts she has gathered to sell.

> REBECCA
> The boy done went into my walnuts!
> I skin my fingers to the bone to
> pick two pounds that's worth almost
> nothin' at the commissary and he done
> took almost half of what I pick!

> NATHAN LEE
> The boy is hungry, Rebecca.

His words cut through her frustration . . . he
holds her close to him for a moment and then they
break the embrace.

> NATHAN LEE
> Dammit!

> REBECCA
> We been through these off-seasons
> before - we made it.

> NATHAN LEE
> What we make it to? The next sea-
> son to work ourselves to death,
> share croppin' for ol' man Howard,
> so he can get richer and we can't
> even eat when the croppin' time
> is done?

Nathan Lee is a strong man, embittered by the system under
which he must live. His son is so hungry he takes food which would
bring in a little money. It is to be expected that Nathan Lee, impelled
by his bitterness and anger, will be forced into some kind of desperate action which will advance the plot.

"NATURAL" DIALOG

Dialog must *seem* natural. It is almost impossible to duplicate
actual conversation, but it must be made to sound the way people
really talk. For instance, never attempt to write group dialog as it
really sounds when several people are gathered together. The result
is a garbled noise with no single voice being heard. In a dinner scene
there can be the murmur of conversation in the background, but

only one or two voices will be distinctly heard by the audience. This may not seem like reality to you, but it is dramatic reality.

Prostitutes do not talk like dowagers, coal miners have different speech from college professors. If you have in a scene, say, three men —a priest, a drug pusher, and a policeman—it should be clear to the audience with its eyes closed which of the three is speaking, not only from what each says but from his choice of words and idiom.

People do ramble when they speak together, but they should not ramble in your screenplay unless you want to lose your audience. Keep the conversation moving.

Human speech does not flow smoothly from the lips. It is often fragmented. There are many "uh's" and "ah's" and pauses and sighs. There are groans and moans and whistles and gasps that can say volumes. Use them when they are appropriate. In many instances they serve better than a sentence, are more provocative, and give greater impetus to the dialog.

Remember that your characters are visible, so it is unnecessary and unnatural for them to call each other frequently by name.

TEMPO

A thoughtfully constructed script will have its own tempo and changes of tempo or pace which are essential not only to the flow of the drama but to the enjoyment of the audience. This will include pages in which the characters have longer speeches than before—to change the rhythm. Or pages of brief staccato speeches for the same purpose. But they should fall in place naturally, never seem forced.

Dialog should be written so that it needs no parenthetical directions. The words should be so carefully chosen that the needed tempo is clearly indicated.

The beginning writer should avoid monologs delivered by a character who is alone in the scene. This device represents an attempt to get into the character's mind and expose his thoughts to the audience. It is sloppy writing. Whatever is in a character's mind must be revealed through other means, some action that illuminates it or dialog with another character.

CONSISTENCY

Never present a character who is one kind of person and have him/her speak like another. An example:

Two slatterns, beer cans in hands, call to each other across a backyard fence on a sweltering summer's day.

>   FIRST SLATTERN
> How are you this morning, Miss Tilley?
> Warm day, isn't it?

>   SECOND SLATTERN
> Indeed it is. And I'm well, thank you.
> How are you?

These neighbors would never address each other in that manner. Their speech is too formal, too restrained. In short, too dead. It gives no indication of their relationship or, more important, of their personalities. It might go like this:

>   FIRST SLATTERN
> Gonna be a booger today, huh? Hotter'n
> a whore's ass.

>   SECOND SLATTERN
> Git on over here and we'll keep the cans
> a-poppin'. That oughta cool us down
> some.

Now it is clear, with very little additional dialog, the kind of women these are and their relationship to each other.

Never use a word that your character would not use. And never use one that does not say exactly what you mean it to say.

An example from *The Godfather* is the scene in which Bonasera, whose daughter has been beaten and almost raped, comes to Don Corleone, the godfather, asking for revenge on the men who did it, after the court has freed them.

In a scene like this, a desperate father might say: "Two bastards tried to rape my daughter, and the judge let them go. She's a good girl and I want revenge." That says it all, doesn't it?

The actual dialog reads:

                         BONASERA
        I raised my daughter in the American
        fashion. She went out with young men
        who tried to dishonor her. They
        beat her. And now the judge has set
        them free. I come to you for my
        justice.

This is the speech of an uneducated man of Italian descent, who speaks with a semblance of Old World reticence. It rings true. In the presence of the revered godfather, he does not speak the word "rape." He uses "dishonor," both out of deference to Don Corleone and out of respect for his daughter. He uses "justice" instead of "revenge" since, in his mind, it is justice that has been denied him, though it is actually revenge he seeks. One of the strongest words in this brief speech is "my." He wants not only justice, but "my" justice.

Another example is the scene from *Sounder* in which Rebecca talks to her preacher about her husband, who has been sent to a county work farm for stealing meat for his hungry family. The preacher asks her not to be bitter and to remember that no matter what her misery is, she must stay with God.

Another woman might have said, "I'll try to remember that, Preacher, but it's hard to do, and my husband is the only one who can help me forgive the injustice that's been done us."

The actual dialog reads:

                         REBECCA
        Yeah, he'll crawl into my bed tonight,
        lie close to my body and keep me warm -
        and rectify the evil in the men who live
        over us in this valley.

That speech is Rebecca. It comes from an ardent, lusty, and bitter woman whose considerable mettle is aroused through her grief and despair. "Rectify" is a superb choice. It is consistent with the vocabulary of a southern black woman with a retentive memory for the strong words that she has heard in church and courthouse. It would be impossible to find words that state as powerfully the oppression under which she lives as "the evil in the men who live over us in this valley." Its truth is harsh, and its poetry and rhythm are pleasant to the ear. (This is a rhetorical statement, since her husband is still in prison.)

The *right* words—those are the only ones you want. Search for them.

STYLE

Style is the way a writer writes. There are many kinds of styles and many variations of them among screenwriters. We think of Woody Allen and Mel Brooks as humorists, yet we would have difficulty comparing *Play It Again, Sam* with *Blazing Saddles* except to say that they are both very funny films. Style does not exist for its own sake, regardless of its appeal. It is the way a writer says something.

In screenwriting, your style must be judged by its relevance to the drama. The drama, after all, is the main dish; style is the way it is prepared and served. It is less important to consider the artistic value of your words than the way those words serve your script. Remember that your originality, your style, cannot be concerned only with the dialog but must also be concerned with the narrative. The narrative in a screenplay precedes a scene or shot and describes the setting, objects to be featured in it, the characters (if not introduced before), and the action.

IMITATION

There is only one thing to be said about your temptation to write imitations of the successful films you admire: Avoid it.

Consider first the many kinds of films from which you may choose: westerns, comedies, costume or historical films, horror films, science fiction films, contemporary dramas, and their many variations. The combinations are endless and are at your disposal. Whichever you select must be the one to which your own particular style is best suited. Whatever compels you to write must dictate the kinds of writing you do. Your writing must spring from your deepest interests and be the servant of your particular talent.

CLICHES

Clichés in screenwriting can be visual as well as verbal. In fact, some entire plots are clichés, such as the golden-oldie plots of the forties and fifties: boy meets girl—boy loses girl—boy gets girl. With the right approach and inspired direction, this is still a mechanism that works dramatically. *A Man and A Woman* is a prime example. But few directors have the genius of Claude Lelouch.

Avoid the falling-leaf gimmick, used to denote the end of autumn. Or a field of daffodils, to show that spring has come. Or snow drifting by the window; winter is here. And so on. The passage of time can be much more dramatically stated.

As for stage-business clichés: How often have you seen actors, in order to keep busy, light a cigarette or pour a drink? There are many other things a human being can do when conversing, stalling for time, or whatever.

There are hundreds of visual clichés which your years of watching films have made familiar to you. It is possible to avoid most of them if you try to construct each scene so that it will be a fresh experience to the audience.

Avoid clichés in dialog. The sole exception to this admonition is in the dialog of a character who will normally speak in clichés. In *Blazing Saddles* the clichés are deliberate and achieve a remarkably humorous effect.

SYMBOLISM

Symbolism is a statement within a statement. The young girl in a white dress, holding a bouquet of daisies, is more than a character; she is a symbol of innocence. She is also a cliché. But if a four-times divorced woman wears a white bridal gown to her fifth wedding, it makes a definite statement about her personality.

By its very nature, symbolism is an intellectual exercise and, as such, must not be overdone. Audiences are watching the actors and action, listening to the dialog, fitting the scenes to the plot or vice versa, and generally are too preoccupied to have time to wonder: what does that really mean?

IMPORTANCE OF REWRITING

Developing one's style is almost synonymous with rewriting. However, since vitality is a most important factor in dialog, you must revise intelligently. Don't rewrite your dialog into a state of juicelessness. Keep in mind that spontaneity must seem to exist.

Write the narrative passages selectively, too, and be as explicit as you can without belaboring a point.

In fiction writing, words are your only tools. The way you use them is your style. In screenwriting, your tools are words, *plus* sets, props, actors, action—and the way you describe these and use them is your style. The end product will be the combined efforts of the screenwriter, producer, director, cinematographer, set designer, sound and lighting engineers, and many others. But your vision was the beginning of it all.

So be prepared to write slowly, carefully, and with respect for language. Also, prepare to rewrite, and rewrite again. Don't betray the vital impulse which gave birth to your screenplay with sloppy or careless writing. This is particularly true of all drafts written after the completion of the rough draft.

2

How to Write the Screenplay

At this point you have plotted your screenplay. You have decided on the basic theme, the conflicts, the characters, the crises, and the climax. You are champing at the bit, and what you want to know now is how to effectively translate your inner visions into a screenplay which will run 100–150 minutes; how to put on paper what your mind's eye sees and what must be clearly revealed to the studio heads, the director, and the actors—and, finally, to the audience.

But wait. First, there is the imperative need to organize all those ideas that are tumbling around in your mind. Before you write a single word of your rough draft, be sure that your play's plot foundation is solid, your framework sound, and your overall story line exactly what you intended it to be.

ORGANIZATION

Before you begin to organize your scenes, it is a good idea to write a *treatment* of your story. A treatment is a detailed summary of the plot, 15–45 pages long. What it covers depends upon the demands of your material. It includes descriptions of characters as they first appear. It can also include scene descriptions, some action, some random dialog, and occasionally some camera angles. In it you tell your story as if you were telling it to a friend: what happens, then what happens next. Remember to keep the treatment trimmed to the essentials of plot and characterizations. And make it as interesting as possible. Whether you submit it by itself or with your completed screenplay, much will depend on it. It is always written in the present tense as if it were being recorded by a camera. See chapter 6 for the first pages of a treatment of *Katie's Ladies* (screenplay by Constance Nash) that will show you exactly how it is set up, what it must include, and the tempo it sets for the ensuing narrative.

An *outline* is a 7-to-12-page description of your play, its plot and major characters. Naturally it cannot be as extensive as a treatment and does not include any specifics, such as the treatment does. It must be written so that the protagonist is made interesting immediately and the conflict/problem is clearly stated within the first page or two. A *synopsis* is only one or two paragraphs, a bare-bones description of the plot such as might be written by a magazine film critic.

An outline of the Cinderella story would begin:

CINDERELLA, a pretty young girl dressed in blue-faded-to-gray rags, is on her knees scrubbing the hearth in the drawing room of what is obviously a wealthy household. Her TWO UGLY STEPSISTERS, their squat figures bulging in satin gowns made ludicrous with coy ruffles and ribbons, are sipping tea and discussing the grand ball which will be held that night at the royal palace. They are all a-twitter because the kingdom's HANDSOME YOUNG PRINCE will not only attend the ball but will choose his bride from among the ladies assembled.

"I would give everything I own to attend such a ball," Cinderella says.

One stepsister brays, "Since all you own are the rags on your back and the cinders in your hair, you don't have much to bargain with, do you?"

The other stepsister caws, "A scullery maid like you? The Prince would have you driven from the palace grounds."

This outline introduces Cinderella, the protagonist; the conflict between her and her family; and the pivotal character, the Prince. It also introduces the element of suspense. Will her stepsisters relent and permit Cinderella to go to the ball? Will she sneak out and peek through the palace windows? What *will* she do?

A synopsis of *Chinatown* would be written: A mystery in which a brash private detective is employed by a beautiful young woman to solve a murder and discovers that he is trapped in a House of Mirrors in which nothing is as it seems. Set in Los Angeles in the 1930s.

Using the treatment as the skeleton of your play, you now begin fleshing out its bones by blocking in its many scenes. One technique for organizing them is to use lined index cards. Write each scene on a card, along with salient fragments of action or dialog that pertain to that scene. On each card, as you introduce a new character or setting, jot down a brief description. Later these scenes will be filled out to form your shot-by-shot sequences or master scenes, but do not worry about that now.

Tack the cards on a cork board in the sequence which seems logical and workable to you. Instead of index cards you can use a blackboard or typing paper, but if your plot is convoluted in design, the index cards are easier to rearrange.

As you write your script, other scenes will come to mind, and other snatches of dialog or objects that are essential to them. Example: if you want to indicate that a character has been outdoors when he insists he has not, simply write "muddy shoes" on the card for that scene.

Another example of how the cards will be of benefit: Suppose you have a character who is an illegitimate child. Do you reveal it right away, or do you save it for heightened shock value later on? You write this scene on a card and move it around until you are certain it is being used to its fullest dramatic effect.

THREE ACTS

In chapter 1 you were given a diagram illustrating how the screenplay can be divided into three acts. The acts are not indicated in your script, but it will be helpful if you have them in mind, to facilitate your plot structuring.

Act 1—contains the conflict or action that rises to a crisis and sets up the sharp confrontation(s) in act 2.

Act 2—the action which ends with the hero/heroine involved in what seems to be an unsolvable problem.

Act 3—the resolution of all conflicts, rising to a satisfactory climax.

These divisions are not ironclad rules. By its nature as a highly creative medium, film writing often departs from traditional formats. For instance, *Nashville* was written in a horizontal manner, without regard for specific acts.

LENGTH OF ACTS

Your script can be anywhere from 100 to 150 pages long, though *120 pages is the preferred length*. A good way to divide the acts into lengths which will best serve your structure is: act 1, approximately one-fourth of the total length; act 2, approximately one-half of the total; and act 3, approximately one-fourth of the total. "Approximately" means that the length may range anywhere from one to ten pages off the precise mark. However, you will find in timing the movies you see that these divisions invariably hold true, give or take a few minutes.

QUESTIONS TO BE ANSWERED

Now ask yourself these questions:

Is my protagonist interesting—will the audience really care about him/her? Does he act, or is he simply acted upon? Is my antagonist strong? Will the readers—producer, director, actors—be intrigued by my script within the first eight to fifteen pages? Have I captivated my readers/audience with a provocative opening scene which serves as a lead-in to the major problem/conflict that besets my characters? (Probably no clearer example of this can be found than in the first six pages of Ernest Lehman's *The Sound of Music* shooting script, which is included in chapter 6.) Have I made a lucid statement of the problem/conflict within the first few pages? Have I built the plot carefully on the cards and in the treatment, so that I know exactly where it is going—exactly what the climax is—and how I will arrange and build the crises that lead into it? Is my drama truly dramatic?

SCREENPLAY STYLES

There are two styles in which screenplays are written: *shot-by-shot* sequences (similar to a shooting script) and *master scenes*. Some writers use both in a single script, depending on where each style best serves the visual content. You may use either technique to the exclusion of the other if it works best for the script, but if you do combine them, do so with caution. Don't jumble them so that the script becomes confusing. There is no single way to write a script, but it must be visually precise. As the highly successful screenwriter Ernest Lehman says in his interview in chapter 4, "I want it written with clarity so that the director, actors, and so forth know what is intended." The key to excellence in screenwriting: what is intended must be clearly stated.

SHOT-BY-SHOT TECHNIQUE

Basically the film shown on the big screen is composed of several thousand feet of *frames,* which are spliced, edited, and run on reels to make the moving pictures. A frame is the square which the camera discloses, similar to a snapshot. It has definite boundaries. Written in the narrative it might read: "John looking out of the frame toward . . ." or "Half an umbrella showing in frame." It can also be used to identify the shot when the script is written in the master scene technique.

The frames are referred to as shots. You must be able to visualize your story scene by scene and, above all, be able to identify the subject of each shot.

The shot-by-shot technique is a form of screenwriting which is done in a clear, unencumbered style. It enables a reader to grasp easily the content of the script by following the capitalized shots, without having to rely solely on the narrative or dialog. A shot is the specific picture on the screen. Movies, whether written in the shot-by-shot technique or in master scenes, are always filmed in shots. (See excerpts from the shooting script of *The Sound of Music* in chapter 6.)

Do not number the shots in your speculative script. Some writers do this, but we feel that it adds nothing to the reader's knowledge and, in any event, the script will not be filmed exactly as the shot numbers indicate. (The shots in *The Sound of Music* are numbered because it is an actual shooting script on which the director worked with the screenwriter.)

The *subject of the shot* is the object on which the camera is focused. It can be an Indian on horseback, a couple lying on the beach, a dog, a signpost, anything that dominates the shot and on which the audience is meant to concentrate. It is identified in capitals and followed either by dialog or the narrative describing the action that takes place in the scene. Whenever the camera moves to focus on something different—setting, object, actor, whatever—it must be clearly identified as a new shot. This makes the instruction CUT TO unnecessary since the camera *must* move with each new shot identified.

Remember that a camera shot is similar to an Instamatic snapshot. Suppose you snap a picture of an Indian chief astride his horse and in the background there is an Indian village. The subject of the shot would be SITTING BULL. In your film script it would be written this way, followed by the descriptive narrative:

SITTING BULL

posing majestically astride his horse. He is wearing full battle dress and a long feathered war bonnet. In the b.g. (background) we see teepees, squaws leaning over adobe ovens, children and dogs running around.

Examples of how the subject of the shot is correctly identified can be found in the following pages from Robert Towne's script of *Chinatown*. (Also see excerpt in chapter 6.)

Note in number 23 how the shot might have been identified as MULWRAY—RIVERBED; but since the focus is on Gittes, the shot is written WITH GITTES. In number 26 the focus is on Mulwray rather than Gittes, so it is identified MULWRAY. In number 31 the camera leaves the two men and concentrates on the park; the subject of the shot becomes POINT FERMIN PARK—DUSK.

23 WITH GITTES

holding a pair of binoculars, downstream and just above the flood control road using some dried mustard weeds for cover. He watches while Mulwray makes his way down to the center of the riverbed.

CONTINUED

23 CONTINUED:

There Mulwray stops, turns slowly, appears to be
looking at the bottom of the riverbed, or at nothing.

24 GITTES

trains the binoculars on him. Sun glints off Mulwray's glasses.

25 BELOW GITTES

There's the SOUND of something like champagne
corks popping. Then a small Mexican boy atop a sway-
back horse rides into the river, and into Gittes'
view.

26 MULWRAY

himself stops, stands still when he hears the
sound. Power lines and the sun are overhead, the
trickle of brackish water at his feet.

He moves swiftly downstream in the direction of the
sound, toward Gittes.

27 GITTES

moves a little farther back as Mulwray rounds the
bend in the river and comes face to face with the
Mexican boy on the muddy banks. Mulwray says something to the boy.

The boy doesn't answer at first. Mulwray points to
the ground. The boy gestures. Mulwray frowns. He
kneels down in the mud and stares at it. He seems to
be concentrating on it.

28 After a moment, he rises, thanks the boy and heads
swiftly back upstream scrambling up the bank to his
car. There he reaches through the window and pulls
out a roll of blueprints or something like them he
spreads them on the hood of his car and begins to
scribble some notes, looking downstream from time
to time.

CONTINUED

28 CONTINUED:

The power lines overhead HUM.

He stops, listens to them then rolls up the plans and gets back in the car. He drives off.

29 GITTES

hurries to get back to his car. He gets in and gets right back out. The steamy leather burns him. He takes a towel from the back seat and carefully places it on the front one. He gets in and takes off.

30 OMITTED

31 POINT FERMIN PARK DUSK

Street lights go on.

32 MULWRAY

pulls up, parks. Hurries out of the car, across the park lawn and into the shade of some trees and build-ings.

33 GITTES

pulls up, moves across the park at a different angle, but in the direction Mulwray had gone. He makes it through the trees in time to see Mulwray scramble adroitly down the side of the cliff to the beach below. He seems in a hurry. Gittes moves after him having a little more difficulty negotiating the climb than Mulwray did.

34 DOWN ON THE BEACH

Gittes looks to his right where the bay is a long, clear crescent. He looks to his left there's a prom-ontory of sorts. It's apparent Mulwray has gone that way. Gittes hesitates, then moves in that di-rection but climbs along the promontory in order to be above Mulwray.

35 AT THE OUTFALL

Gittes spots Mulwray just below him, kicking at the sand.

                                    CONTINUED

Though, as mentioned earlier in this chapter, the actual instruction CUT TO is seldom used, the ability of a camera to cut from one shot to another is one of the most valuable techniques of film writing and film making. It gives the film great forward mobility, swiftly and smoothly moving the action along.

Example: In their living room, a man asks his wife if she would like to go to the beach. Immediately the script (and the camera) has them lying on beach towels beside the ocean. The audience is spared the tedium of their packing their swim suits and suntan lotion, getting into the car, and driving to the beach. The man's wish instantly becomes reality (an example of the delightful fantasy fulfillments the movies bring us). Today's sophisticated audiences always understand that DISSOLVE means the end of one scene or a change of time or both. Study the excerpts in chapter 6 for scene changes, then note the shot changes within them.

After you have chosen the subject of the camera shot, you must indicate whether the setting is inside or outside and whether it is day or night. This is written INT.—DAY or EXT.—NIGHT. You may, of course, use other designations for day or night, such as dawn, dusk, noon. If it is obvious in the script that the shots following the original designation are taken at the same time there is no need to repeat the instructions.

MASTER SCENE TECHNIQUE

A master scene is one in which all narrative, dialog, and action relative to a single setting is written beneath the initial description of the locale. There are times when you simply will not be able to break a scene into specific camera shots. Within a single scene there may be several interesting camera angles or cuts, but you do not write them. That is left to the director when he works with you or another writer on the final shooting script. (See master scene excerpt on page 138.)

A fine example of a scene which involves too much activity to use the shot-by-shot technique: in *The Godfather* Mario Puzo writes a master scene which takes place in a garden at a wedding. Under EXT. GARDEN WEDDING SCENE the camera explores every corner of the scene, in which there are hundreds of guests. We move among the tables, hear revealing snatches of conversations, go among the guests dancing to a band playing the "Tarantella," watch the wedding photographer taking pictures, and occasionally focus on two or more of the principal characters. During the scene, through dialog and behavior, we learn something interesting about almost all the important characters in the screenplay. It is a colorful scene, filled with activity, and as it progresses there are snatches of clear dialog and some sharp character vignettes. It could never have been written in the shot-by-shot technique.

Remember the difference between a scene and a shot: a scene includes all action and dialog that occurs in one locale; a shot is similar to a snapshot and many of them may be incorporated in a single scene.

Each typed page will run approximately sixty seconds on film, whether it is dialog or narrative. (Therefore, 120 pages=2 hours of film.)

TERMINOLOGY

In making a film the director and actors will be informed and guided by the directions and descriptions contained in the script. These should be complete without redundancy, graphic without excessive detail. Every craft, sport, trade, and profession has developed its own particular terminology which becomes essential for quick communication among its participants. Without a working knowledge of the terminology of screenwriting you will find yourself floundering in confusion.

It is absolutely vital to your understanding of how to write a screenplay that you become thoroughly familiar with screenwriting terms before you tackle your rough draft. Otherwise you cannot hope to bring your screenplay to its complete visual realization.

Below we will give the screenwriter's vocabulary. However, you must remember that it is the mark of the amateur to overuse or incorrectly use camera directions and editing techniques. Those decisions must be left to the director.

There are times in every screenplay when it is imperative to use certain shots, such as POV, CLOSE-UP, LONG SHOT, or PAN, to give dramatic definition to a particular scene. This conveys the specific meaning or intention of the scene to the director.

As an example of, say, a CLOSE-UP shot, you might need to show, for dramatic impact, headlines in a newspaper which a character is reading but which you want the audience to see. It would be written:

CLOSE-UP - NEWSPAPER HEADLINES

Guard Killed in Bank Robbery

Beginning screenwriters often are either frightened by camera instructions and refuse to use them, or enamored of them and use them to excess. If you know how to use the terms properly, you won't be guilty of either.

One last warning: unless the directions are absolutely vital to the director's understanding of the explicit intent of the scene, avoid the unpardonable "directing on paper."

Most of the screenwriting vocabulary can be divided into the following five categories: (1) *Camera angle descriptions:* terms which designate the position and angle of the camera in relation to its subject. (2) *Special effects shots,* an aptly named category that includes the terms needed for camera and editing techniques which provide heightened dramatic effects. (3) *Transitional instructions:* terms used to show how one scene is DISSOLVED or CUT TO another scene. (4) *Subject-in-motion shots,* showing how to indicate whether the camera is stationary or in motion when the subject of the shot is moving. (5) *Audio instructions:* terms used to inject special vocal effects into the script.

There are other terms which defy categorizing but which you will need to become familiar with. These are:

FRAME: A rectangle which the camera discloses, similar to a snapshot. Has definite boundaries.

SHOT: The specific picture on the screen. (Interchangeable with FRAME.)

INTO VIEW: Used when the shot first reveals a portion of the whole and slowly moves to include the rest of the subject. Example: Two people are in bed. First the camera focuses on the wife, then moves to her husband. The directions would read: HUSBAND INTO VIEW. The camera moves to include her husband who is already there. The subject of the shot would be: INT.—NIGHT—BEDROOM. (INTO FRAME means that something new moves into the shot on which the camera is already focused. Example: When the camera is focused on the woman in bed, the man would not be there but would walk into the room—INTO FRAME.)

b.g. (background): Used within the narrative and described in lower-case initials or written in full. It refers to something happening in the background of the shot while attention is focused on the foreground. Example: Two people are lying on the deck of a small boat. In the b.g. we see a large boat bearing down on them.

PAUSE or BEAT: Used to mark a pause in dialog. You can break a character's long speech by inserting (BEAT) or (PAUSE).

CONTINUED: Written under a character's name when his dialog has been interrupted by some action (not by another character speaking) and is continued. Also used in the script when the dialog or scene is continued on the next page. It is typed in caps at the lower right margin of the first page and the upper left margin of the next.

PARENTHETICAL DIRECTIONS: Directions showing how a line is to be delivered or what the character is doing. They appear beneath the character's name, preceding his dialog. These are very brief, so minimal that it is not necessary to make a separate narrative passage of them. They are used only when they are needed to inform an actor or director that they are essential to the *meaning* of the dialog or scene. They are never inserted merely to tell an actor how to deliver the lines; this is both disruptive and unnecessary if your dialog "speaks" for itself, as it should. Examples:

```
              AMELIA
        (dropping her racket)


                 or


         CAPTAIN McWUEEL
          (softly)
     Shape up, soldier, I won't give you
     that order twice.
```

In the first example Amelia's dropping the racket is an important piece of action, but is too brief to require a separate narrative passage. In the second example Captain McWueel's command could have several interpretations. It could have been shouted, snarled, or barked. Spoken softly, however, its effect becomes more deadly, and the instruction was a necessary one.

CAMERA ANGLE DESCRIPTIONS

CLOSE-UP: A shot that emphasizes a detail: for example, a mouth, hand, ball, or signpost.

CLOSE SHOT: Shows a character from the shoulders up and includes some background detail, used often in television. Should not be confused with CLOSE-UP.

MEDIUM SHOT: Shows one or more persons, as in MEDIUM GROUP SHOT. The shot is usually waist high and up. Most directors think in medium shots, so it is not necessary to identify them in your script.

LONG SHOT: The next shot after the MEDIUM SHOT. It includes the entire body or bodies and more detail of the scene. It is also used to reveal a wide area or a far distance.

EXTREME LONG SHOT (XLS):   Encompasses considerable distance but without definition.

WIDE ANGLE: A variation on the long shot in which a special camera lens is used. It includes more on the sides than an ordinary shot. (A wide angle might be used to photograph an entire amphitheater.)

PAN: The camera is mounted on a pedestal and its head moves from left to right or right to left. For instance, it PANS an audience, showing many faces but stopping on none.

ZOOM: The camera pulls rapidly forward, enlarging the subject. Example: Camera ZOOMS in on a diamond ring.

TILT SHOT: The camera can tilt up or down, giving emphasis to a certain object in the scene. Examples: TILT UP to a figure on a cliff top; TILT DOWN to muddy shoes.

ANGLE ON: Another camera view of a previous shot. Used to emphasize a specific thing in the scene, such as ANGLE ON GIRL looking through a fence.

REVERSE ANGLE: A shot 180 degrees opposite of the one that preceded it. It alternates between two important subjects, such as two faces in a passionate confrontation. It is not necessary to indicate it if you write in the shot-by-shot technique.

SPECIAL EFFECTS SHOTS

INSERT: Used to show some detail that is not included in the scene but that is important to it. Example: You are describing a battle scene during the Mexican-American War and you want to show a map of the territory over which the fighting is taking place. You write:

INSERT - MAP

of Mexico 1831

The map is not part of the scene which the camera is shooting; it is simply inserted for a moment, then withdrawn. This is not to be confused with a CLOSE-UP of something the camera is already recording. For instance, a man is reading a newspaper, and the next shot shows a CLOSE-UP of the story he is reading. That is a CLOSE-UP of something already in the scene, not something which is inserted.

POV: Abbreviation for *point of view*. It is a cinematic trick used to present a scene so that the audience sees it through the eyes of a particular character. More than that, it is a means for transmitting the character's emotional response so clearly that the audience must feel the same response. Example: It is an early evening in summer and a pretty girl is sitting on a park bench, reading. A man approaches and she looks up. He could be a pleasant man who simply wants to be friendly. But you take the audience into the girl's mind from her POV—and show through her eyes the man's evil and demented face, which arouses immense fear in her. The audience's emotional response will be in accord with hers. (The emotion called for need not always be as strong as fear. It can be gentle yet positive, such as sudden delight or enormous relief.) Example:

GIRL'S POV

of a leering mad man as he slowly reaches with his
right hand into an inside pocket of his filthy
coat.

POV can also be used to show the point of view of the subject
of the shot. For instance, the POV of a car on a dirt road could
be written:

CADILLAC POV

as the twin headlights cut through the steadily
thickening fog, revealing a narrow road ahead.

We know we are looking into the fog from the viewpoint of the
car but not necessarily from the POV of the driver. The audience is made to feel that it is inside the car, looking out.

REVERSE POV: The POV shot reversed to show the original
subject. Example: We see through the eyes of the leering man
in the park as he leans over the cowering girl. It is written:
REVERSE POV—MAN.

OVER THE SHOULDER SHOT: We see the back of the subject's
head from the shoulders up in the foreground while the camera
focuses on a specific thing in the background. We know that the
object is seen by the character in the foreground. Example:

PARSONS – OVER THE SHOULDER

Favoring Jessica and Audrey as they leave the car
and slowly walk up the drive, dawdling along the
way. Jessica looks up, sees Parsons, and smiles. He
raises a hand in greeting.

We know from this that the audience will see Parsons' shoulder
and the back of his head. We will see what he sees when Jessica
smiles. And we will see his hand raised to greet her. ("Favoring" means the person or thing on which the camera is focused
in the background.)

SERIES OF SHOTS: Literally a series of shots, run one after
another. Used to indicate the passage of time, stream of con-
sciousness, separate but related events leading up to a climactic

scene. Example: SERIES OF SHOTS—INDIANAPOLIS 500.

SLOW MOTION: The slowing down of the camera. Used to create tension, as in a slow-motion shot of a long-distance runner as he makes great long strides toward the finish line. Use this shot as a chef uses his strongest spices—with extreme caution.

AERIAL SHOT: Used if necessary to indicate a shot taken from a plane (not a crane) looking down on the scene. Example: AERIAL SHOT—SIXTH FLEET, PORT OF SAN DIEGO.

ESTABLISHING SHOT: Compilation of shots which establishes the primary locale of the film. Usually good for the opening of a film. To establish Washington, D.C., there would be a long shot of Pennsylvania Avenue leading up to a full view of the White House.

SPLIT SCREEN SHOT: Used to show two separate subjects of the shot on screen simultaneously. For instance, two people are talking to each other on the phone and you want to show the reactions of both.

FREEZE FRAME: The picture stops moving, becomes a still photograph, and holds for a period of time.

MONTAGE: A sequence of shots similar to a SERIES OF SHOTS. The difference is that more is shown on the screen at the same moment. For instance, two or more different subjects can be blended at the same time like a montage painting. It can be surrealistic or impressionistic. Rarely used.

STOCK SHOT: Films of events photographed in the past that are canned and stored in Hollywood. There is stock footage on all recent wars, airplanes flying in formation, aerial shots of islands or the English Channel, marching bands, animal stampedes. (In *Baa Baa Black Sheep,* the aerial action shots are STOCK SHOTS.) This is where you exercise your awareness of film budgeting.

SUPER: Abbreviation for *superimpose.* The superimposition of one thing over another in the same shot. Sometimes TITLES are superimposed over scenes. Or a face can be superimposed over a stream-of-consciousness montage shot.

TRANSITIONAL INSTRUCTIONS

Transitional instructions, such as DISSOLVE, FADE IN, or CUT TO, are editing techniques and generally are to be avoided. (In television scripts, however, they are frequently used.) Leave these directions to the director. If you feel they are necessary to stress a particular point, be very circumspect in using them.

FADE IN: A process in which the picture emerges from a darkened screen to a fully lighted screen. Traditionally it is used to open the movie, though in rare instances it is used to incorporate a new scene which has to be set apart from the immediate action—such as fantasy, a daydream, or a flashback. Because fades are an editing technique, you do not have to be overly concerned with them. In television scripts they are commonly used to open and close each act.

FADE OUT: The same process in reverse. The screen gradually darkens to black, literally fading out the picture. Traditionally used to end the movie.

CROSSFADE: Fading out of one scene as it darkens and the fading in of another as it lightens. It is not to be confused with DISSOLVE, since CROSSFADE always involves a black or blank screen.

DISSOLVE: Used as a time lapse not to be confused with cutting from shot to shot. A *blending* of two shots achieved by the simultaneous fading out of one image (the screen darkens) and the fading in of another image in reverse density of dark to medium. The first picture disappears into the next picture. It involves the merging of two pictures and never the use of a blank screen or dark screen. Often used in treatments to indicate the passage of time. Example: We DISSOLVE to the bordello.

CUT TO: The abrupt ending of one scene and the beginning of another. It is the common transition between scenes. As we have said, writing CUT TO in your script is generally redundant since there is no way to shoot the next subject of the shot without cutting to it. But it is necessary if you are writing exclusively in master scenes. Occasionally you might want to employ a tricky cut, such as INTER-CUT, in which case it would be specifically designated. CUT TO is often used in writing treatments.

CUTAWAY SHOT: Used to take attention away from the primary action for a moment. It can establish a plot point or focus on a subplot facet to give drama or tension to the scene. Use sparingly.

INTER-CUT: The interfacing of two scenes meant to be one scene. It can be used effectively to show what is happening simultaneously between two subjects. Example: A scene of a man and a woman talking to each other on the telephone. It can be INTER-CUT from the man to the woman, showing their emotions. Or lovemaking scenes between two couples in different locations can be INTER-CUT, though the voices of only one couple are VOICED-OVER during the INTER-CUT scenes.

MATCH CUT: A matching of the subject of a shot in one scene with a similar subject in the next scene. Example: Cover of a book showing a photograph of a Corsair airplane against a blue sky. MATCH CUT to a real Corsair against a blue sky.

Subject-in-Motion Shots

These shots can be handled in two ways: either with the camera moving on wheels or with the camera remaining stationary. Both record the considerable movement of the subject of the shot. The rule is: if it is necessary to *accompany* the moving subject in order to see or feel something that enhances the drama of the scene, then designate it as a moving shot. Conversely, the stationary camera photographs the subject as it is in motion but does not accompany the subject.

Examples of properly designated moving shots:

PARSONS IN CAR – MOVING

along a dirt road. It is dawn and the shadows make it difficult to see well. He stops at a fork in the road trying to decide which route to take. (The camera is mounted on a truck and moving along with Parsons.)

FARTHER UP – MOVING

more slowly as the road narrows. In the b.g. he can see what appears to be smoke rising from a chimney.

Examples of shots in which the subject moves but the camera does not:

```
EXT. CADILLAC - LONG SHOT

The land is barren, dusty. The road winds through
endless honey-hued hillocks which fade into the
horizon. The car passes on.

INT. CADILLAC - PARSONS

rummaging through the lighted glove compartment
for flask - looks up in time to avoid ramming the
right side of a cement bridge abutment.
```

(Interior shots which show two people in a vehicle can be photographed with a stationary camera as the scenery flashes by on a screen behind the vehicle. Commonly used in television as a PROCESS SHOT.)

TRAVELING SHOT: A shot in which the camera is mounted on a dolly and moves with the walking subject of the shot. Example: pages 4–6 of Ernest Lehman's screenplay *The Sound of Music,* in chapter 6. If your subject is simply walking from one room to the next it is not necessary to indicate a TRAVELING SHOT. The camera doesn't have to move to record it. The character must walk a considerable distance (along a beach, for instance) to warrant a TRAVELING SHOT.

DOLLY UP, DOLLY BACK: As it records, the camera moves toward a subject or back from it. The same as CAMERA UP or CAMERA BACK, which is preferable.

AUDIO INSTRUCTIONS

Sound is engineered to synchronize with the visual effects on the screen and is as important to the film as any other ingredient. Thus, there will be times when you need to incorporate special sound effects into your script.

Sound can be used to spark emotional reactions. Go over your script and determine where an effect can be heightened by the use of sound, whether the reaction is meant to be one of fear or joy or shock. The imaginative use of sound can provide color or suspense or both.

O.S.:   Abbreviation for OFF-SCREEN and the audio instruction used most often. The sound is coming from someone OFF-SCREEN while the camera is focused on someone or something else. For that shot the OFF-SCREEN actor's dialog is written under his name and in parentheses is written (O.S.) just above his dialog. OFF-SCREEN action which is indicated by sound is written into the narrative. Example: A frightened child who is hiding hears the (O.S.) footsteps of her kidnapper as they get louder and louder.

VOICE-OVER: To be used sparingly. It is written (V.O.) and means that a voice (or song) is heard over the action on the screen. Example of a V.O. technique: we see German troops goose-stepping, children being herded into bomb shelters, soldiers diving into foxholes, while at the same time we *hear* the impassioned speech of a demagogue. Or we may hear a letter being read aloud, but we do not see either the letter or the person reading it; instead we may see a funeral cortege in another place and time, which has a direct bearing on what we hear.

The difference between OFF-SCREEN and VOICE-OVER is that the person or thing making an (O.S.) sound can be immediately photographed by the camera since it is concurrent with the scene being shot, whereas the (V.O.) sound, such as a song, a speech, or a letter being read, cannot be photographed by the camera as it is a sound effect dubbed over a scene.

ROUGH DRAFT

A rough draft is just what the name implies. It is the first off-the-top rendition of your screenplay, and it is never submitted for consideration by an agent or producer/director. Follow the advice of Ingmar Bergman, who said in a recent interview that movies are "the most fascinating medium in the world. Like music we go straight to the feelings. Afterward we can work with our intellects. But first the feelings."

EXPOSITION

Exposition is the exposure of facts or ideas. In screenwriting, all expositions naturally must be accomplished through dialog and action since, unlike the novelist, the writer cannot simply tell what has gone on before. And this is the way exposition is used in a screenplay —to convey what has happened, either before a particular scene or before the screenplay itself began. Sometimes the latter can be achieved by a narrator, as the film fades in, explaining events that have led up to the current situation. This, however, is frowned upon as being too much like the outmoded butler-and-maid dialog in the opening moments of a stage play which became a theatrical cliché when used to set the scene.

Skillful exposition is so smoothly injected in a screenplay that the audience is unaware that it is being fed hard facts in order to bring it up to date. This calls for much subtlety and inventiveness on your part.

Never deliver facts so that they seem to have been dragged in by their heels, such as a character's monolog describing previous events or a scene in which your only purpose is to establish a single fact.

In his interview in chapter 4, Ernest Lehman says, "I think another bit of advice I would give [to beginning writers], whether it is needed or not, is: be aware of the difficulties of conveying exposition. Try to spoon-feed exposition in such a way that it is palatable, so that it doesn't *seem* to be exposition. Try to work it into a scene that has a little bit of conflict so that the character seems to be *forced* to say what he's saying, rather than conveniently saying it to achieve the writer's end."

Be stealthy about your exposition. Sneak it in so that it becomes fact before the audience is aware of it.

An example of how to use exposition in dialog: A wagon master approaches a gloomy young man who is leaning against his wagon.

                    WAGON MASTER
          How is she?

                    YOUNG MAN
          Not so good.

                         WAGON MASTER
          I swore I'd never let another pregnant
          woman join this wagon train.

                          YOUNG MAN
          Well, at least we mind our own business,
          which is more than I can say for some
          folks on this train.

                         WAGON MASTER
          You mean the Weltons?

                          YOUNG MAN
          I sure in hell do.

Without a scene between the young man and his wife we know that she is having a difficult pregnancy. We know that the wagon master expects it to cause trouble for the train, perhaps by delaying its progress. We know, too, without a scene to explain it, that there is bad blood between the young couple and the Welton family. So in this brief exchange (only 48 words of dialog) we are made fully aware that there are two problems confronting the wagon master, problems that must be resolved before the screenplay ends.

In your local library you will find volumes of plays by the greatest playwrights, living and dead, which you can study to learn how exposition is handled by the masters. Among the moderns, perhaps the best examples can be found in the works of Arthur Miller, Tennessee Williams, William Inge, Paddy Chayevsky, and Neil Simon.

First the Feelings

You are ready to write the rough draft. So open the tap and let it flow. Remember: first the feelings. Don't worry about literary quality. Always mindful of your intent to create a visual as well as an audible experience for the audience, write without revisions or polishing. Don't worry about being shallow or heavy or obvious. If something seems wrong or inconsistent, leave it and plow right along. Beginners are inclined to become discouraged when something doesn't jell properly. Don't let this bother you. Finish your script. Bring it to the climax you have chosen for it. Then stop and take some time off to go to the movies.

It is imperative at this point to put your script away for a few weeks. Don't pick it up again until you feel that you have acquired some degree of objectivity toward it. Its weaknesses and faults will be clearer to you now, and you will be better able to rework them for your second draft.

Use your movie-going experience to advantage. Watch the films conscientiously, and time them with your watch. Note the length of the scenes and the specific subject of the shot changes within each of them. Consider how the scenes flow into each other, and how they, in turn, rise to crises and intensify to the climax at the end. A good thing to look out for is the *length* of each scene. Usually they run no longer than four minutes, each one representing a change in time or place or action. Time the action sequences with or without dialog. Study them until you begin to feel the tempo and rhythm of the film. Look for POV, CLOSE, MEDIUM, and LONG SHOTS. Listen to the dialog to learn how it is used for exposition and for character delineation.

BE BELIEVABLE

Always strive for credibility. To facilitate plotting by asking the audience to believe the unbelievable is slovenly and, in the end, a negation of your intention—which is to use the magic of the medium to spellbind your audience. If anything on the screen makes them say, "Oh, come now. Who could possibly believe that?" the spell is broken. (Exceptions: fantasies or sci-fi movies in which the audience is expected to suspend disbelief.)

For instance, a man dashes into his home, his clothes are torn, and blood seeps from many wounds. He clings to his wife as she tenderly washes and bandages him, but says he cannot talk about it. She accepts this temporarily, and since he is hysterical, this is believable. But if three months later she says to him, "You never told me what happened that night. Will you tell me now," that is definitely not believable. Perhaps you need his disclosure to be delayed for purposes of plot development, but no one will believe that such a close and loving couple would not have discussed his beating before this.

Or his being hit by a truck. Or clawed by a tiger. No wife would be able to bear the suspense for more than a day or two.

Check for loopholes in the plot that will strain the credulity of the audience. Do not give them a reason to say to themselves, "That's ridiculous. Why didn't he simply do thus-and-so?"

Suppose you have an organized-crime chieftain concocting an elaborate scheme to frame a small-time hood for larceny. This is done, the audience is told, because the hood has seen the crime boss commit a murder. Why, the audience will ask itself, doesn't the boss simply have the hood gunned down? Unless it is made clear that the hood has given an incriminating letter to his attorney, to be opened in the event of his premature demise, no one will believe that a man who deals with his enemies by murdering them would go to such elaborate lengths to have an insignificant one merely sent to prison.

REWRITING

Now you are back at your desk, ready slowly and painstakingly to write the second draft. First the feelings, now the intellect. This is not the draft which will be submitted to your agent or to a director or producer. You will want to rewrite it several times before you are satisfied that all the elements involved in plot, characterization, and dialog are as interesting, taut, and finely balanced as you can make them. If the moviemakers are sufficiently interested, you may be asked to make revisions or, if the script is bought or optioned, you may be paid to rewrite it to include the suggestions of the director, producer, or story editor. It is extremely rare for a novice writer to be assigned to write the shooting script.

Now you begin to rewrite, to make deletions and additions, to search for the right word, the telling gesture, the imaginative audio and visual effects. Now is the time to be absolutely certain about the subjects of the shots and have them clearly identified. Remember, a screenplay is a blueprint for a movie. Write so that the reader will be able to visualize your script with ease. No contractor can understand how a structure is to be built without specific blueprints from the architect.

In order to know the correct format for the construction of this important draft and how to give it a professional presentation, you will need to refer often to chapter 3, "Script Format." Explicit instructions will be given on how the dialog and narrative should be presented, as well as on all camera angles.

Put your dialog to the test: Does it reveal the character, is it true of him/her? Is it exactly the way he/she would speak? (Another test of dialog: Do you need it? Would what it says be better "spoken" through action? Or through some other human sound—a groan, a giggle—that is not dialog?)

Ask yourself these questions: Do the action and dialog have balance? Is the action overshadowed by lengthy dialog (a common failing of novice screenwriters)? Is everything—dialog, sound, visuals—indispensable to the delineation and impetus of the plot? Are more of these techniques needed? Are the crises sharp? Is the climax inevitable but not predictable? Is the conflict so strong that the audience really cares about "what happens next"? Is there enough tension, not only between characters but in the situations that involve them? If the screenplay is a comedy, is there enough spontaneity and sense of the absurd to sweep the audience along in the fun?

Your film must be *visual first, verbal second.* One of the most important techniques is the use of action to substitute for dialog. What characters do can, as in "real" life, speak louder about their motivations and intentions than what they say. The way two people run toward each other on a rainy street, stop, hesitate, then move forward and lock arms, can substitute for several lines of dialog. A safe rule to follow: use action to speak for your characters as often as you can. Keep your motion picture in motion.

You have been given the vocabulary and definitions of various camera angles and transitional instructions. You must know them and how to use them, *but use them as little as possible.* Excessive reliance on them is, in fact, detrimental to your script. Use them only when you believe they are absolutely essential to the scene. This will give the director confidence in your ability to understand his prerogatives and also in your knowledge of how to use the tools of screenwriting with precision and sensitivity.

Keep in mind that your screenplay is the key to the power of the production.

KEEP IN MIND:

Within the first 8 to 15 pages the protagonist(s) and the conflict/problem must be introduced and made interesting.

One typed page usually equals one minute of playing time.

Most scenes run no more than two minutes and should never exceed four minutes.

A treatment is approximately 15 to 45 pages in length.

An outline is 7 to 12 pages long.

A synopsis is one or two paragraphs.

Learn to identify the subject of each shot accurately.

Write your rough draft with feeling; your other drafts with your intellect.

Do not permit your protagonist to be the passive victim of events. He must act, not simply be acted upon.

Have the climax in mind before committing anything to paper.

Allow ten months to a year for the writing.

Keep the script moving.

Don't direct on paper.

3

Script Format

As you begin writing your last draft, which may be your third, fourth, or fifth draft, another important facet of screenwriting will concern you: How do you make your typed script look professional?

Here again, there are no absolute rules concerning the format in which a film script is typed. We intend to give you general guidelines which will ensure a thoroughly professional appearance for your script.

In chapter 6 you will find slightly different presentations in the scripts, but bear in mind that these are not first or fifth drafts, such as you will be writing. They are shooting scripts and are presented here in their actual formats. You will not be writing a shooting script.

SCRIPT TITLE PAGE

Drop twenty single spaces from the top of the page and type your title in the center of the page. It must be in caps, bracketed in quotes, and underlined.

Drop another four spaces and type, in caps and lower case: Written by, Screenplay by, an Original Screenplay by, or Created by—whichever applies to your particular script. It is centered on the page.

Drop another two spaces beneath this and type your name in caps and lower case, also centered.

Title pages vary according to the source or origin of your screenplay material. If it is based on a novel, play, or short story by another author, drop eight spaces beneath your name and type: Based on the novel "Such and Such." Drop another two spaces and type: by. Drop two more spaces and type the author's name. This same format is used if your script is based on characters from another source. Instead of typing: Based on the novel by, etc., you type: Based on characters from, etc. All lines are written in caps and lower case.

In the lower left corner type the number of the draft, whether First, Second, or Third Draft. Single-spaced beneath it, type the date.

In the lower right corner type your name, address, and phone number, or those of your agent. These are also single-spaced, in caps and lower case.

In each corner, the top lines should be parallel to each other and end at least two inches above the bottom of the page.

Example of a title page for an original script:

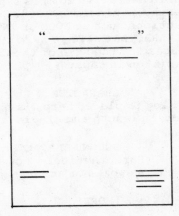

TYPEWRITER SETTINGS

Facilitate your typing by first adjusting your typewriter settings to the seven points which you will use consistently throughout the script. (The top and bottom margins, which cannot be set except in your mind's eye, should each be about one inch deep.)

Tab your settings on these numbers:

Pica type:	17	28	35	43	65	72	75
Elite type:	20	33	42	51	78	87	90

hese are used to indicate:

Left margin: 17 pica, 20 elite
Dialog: 28 pica, 33 elite
Parenthetical directions: 35 pica, 42 elite
Character speaking: 43 pica, 51 elite
Transitional instructions: 65 pica, 78 elite (fades,* dissolve, cut to)
Page number: 72 pica, 87 elite
Right margin: 75 pica, 90 elite

EXAMPLE

SUBJECT OF THE CAMERA SHOT (or scene locale)

Description in narrative form is typed here, two spaces beneath and single-spaced. SOUND and camera directions such as ZOOM or INTO VIEW are in caps. If a CHARACTER EXITS it is also in caps. Drop two spaces for the name of the CHARACTER speaking, written in caps.

CHARACTER
Dialog is placed here, is three inches in length and single-spaced.

SECOND CHARACTER
(Parenthetical - how line is spoken or actor's gestures.)

(MORE)

*Exception: FADE IN and FADE OUT when used only at the beginning and end of the script are written in the left margin.

```
                    SECOND CHARACTER (CONT'D)
                   (gesture: Also includes
                   O.S. and V.O. instructions.)

              Dialog is written here, just as above.

      And if some action interrupts the dialog, that
      action is written into the narrative until the
      action is completed and the script returns to the
      dialog.

                    SECOND CHARACTER (CONT'D)
                   Dialog is resumed after the inter-
                   ruption.

                                      DISSOLVE TO:

      SUBJECT OF THE SHOT or new master scene
```

FORMAT RULES

These words should always be typed in caps: SCENE LOCALE, SUBJECT OF THE SHOT, EXT. and INT., NIGHT, DAY, CHARACTER'S NAME above the dialog, NEW CHARACTER introduced into the narrative, all SOUNDS, CAMERA DIRECTIONS, and SHOTS.

Single-space dialog, narrative, character directions, camera directions, scene descriptions.

Double-space between the speeches of different characters, between the subject of the shot and the character's name, between the narrative description and the character's name, scene, or subject of the shot or camera shot that follows it.

It is important to break a long narrative passage into paragraphs if it begins to crowd the page. So after four or five lines of narrative, double-space and continue with it. Let some light in, leave some white space.

TITLE PAGE FOR TREATMENTS OR OUTLINES

Just as on the screenplay's title page, the title will be centered, in caps, underlined, and bracketed in quotes. Drop four spaces and type, in caps and lower case: Written by. Drop another two spaces and type your name in caps and lower case. Drop two spaces and write the date.

If your treatment or outline is based on another source, such as a novel or a newspaper article, drop eight spaces beneath your name and type the name of the source and the author, if it is known (in newspaper stories the reporter may not have a byline).

The first page after the title page must indicate whether it is a treatment or outline for a screenplay, teleplay, or pilot for a TV series. This will be written at the top of the page, keeping in mind the one-inch margin, and centered with the title in caps and lower case, in quotes, and underlined. Centered two spaces beneath it will be typed: A Treatment of an Original Screenplay; or An Outline for a Two Hour Teleplay; written by, or whatever. (See page 144 for an example.)

Some treatments/outlines are broken into three acts or more and must be designated as such, typed Act One, underlined, written in caps, and set apart from the narrative by double spacing. It is written against the left margin.

If you are writing for a specific television program you will begin the outline, preceding Act One, with a Teaser which will contain the opening scene of the teleplay, the set-up, in approximately two paragraphs.

Remember that a treatment is 15 to 45 pages long, an outline is 7 to 12 pages long.

VARIATIONS FOR TELEVISION FORMATS

Television scripts differ slightly from movie scripts. It would be wise to write to the various shows and request sample scripts, explaining that you are interested in writing a speculation script for them. (Further information on this is given in chapter 5.) Generally, you can be safe in following the instructions given for typing the movie scripts.

Nearly all television scripts begin with a Teaser followed by from two to six acts, depending on the length of the teleplay. The acts are necessitated by breaks for commercials.

Teleplays follow these basic formats:

30-minute teleplay:
    28 to 31 pages; preceded by Teaser of 3 to 7 pages
    Two acts, approximately 13 pages each
60-minute teleplay:
    58 to 61 pages; Teaser of 3 to 9 pages
    Four acts, approximately 14 pages each
90-minute teleplay:
    88 to 90 pages; Teaser of 4 to 9 pages
    Six acts, approximately 14 pages each
120-minute teleplay:
    110 to 120 pages; Teaser of 4 to 10 pages
    Six acts, equally divided after Teaser

Each act should rise to a suspenseful or poignant moment so that the viewers will not be tempted to switch channels during the following station break. These peak points, called "buttons," are necessary in comedies as well as in dramas. You do not need to be concerned about the commercial breaks because, unless you have created a flawless script, it will probably be changed many times prior to shooting.

TAPE FORMAT (THREE-CAMERA TECHNIQUE)

An exception to the basic typing formats given in this chapter is the video-tape or live-tape format using the three-camera technique. These are scripts for the shows which are listed as "Taped" shows in the Writers Guild of America's Television Market List. *Rhoda, The Mary Tyler Moore Show,* and most of the Norman Lear productions are referred to as taped. Scripts for these teleplays are always double-spaced throughout, which makes them approximately 50 percent longer in the number of pages. (See Constance Nash and Virginia Oakey, *The Television Writer's Handbook* [New York: Harper & Row, 1978].)

NUMBER OF SCRIPTS NEEDED

If you do not trust your own typing, have a professional typist make the final presentation copy of your script. If you do this, your instructions must be explicit and leave no room for innovations on the typist's part. You will want a number of copies of your script, so have it copied by Xerox or IBM. If your agent accepts the script, he will need at least six copies. This also applies to your screenplay treatments. Submitting a half-dozen copies is a real time-saver, since it would take years for one script to make the rounds from director to producer to studio heads to actors.

"Spec" scripts—those written on speculation without being assigned or commissioned by a producer or director—are the proof of your screenwriting expertise and must be as clean and readable as possible.

Do not include pictures, maps, sketches, or any extraneous material. Your script must stand on its own without gimmicks.

FOLDERS

The major agencies have their own presentation folders which they will substitute for yours to make sure that the scripts they submit are easily identifiable. However, bind your scripts in inexpensive three-hole folders fastened with brass cotter pins in order to hold the pages together without risk of having a few slide out and into obscurity. In larger cities there are script-binding services which, in addition to professional typing, will provide a three-hole vinyl folder with the title of the screenplay embossed on the cover.

Do not use any other kinds of folders.

Interviews

We have tried to serve as your surrogate as we interviewed the successful film writers, film makers, and film executives for this chapter. The questions we asked were those which, we hope, you would ask if you could sit down with these individuals and put before them the problems which concern you as a novice screenwriter. You will see that the interviewees are not always in total agreement on every issue. Among such creative individuals, in such a creative medium, the probability of agreement would be extremely unlikely. However, there is one point on which they do agree, without exception. That is: writers must write and write and write. Then rewrite and rewrite. An idea or a concept is not enough to prove your seriousness about writing or to provide proof of your talent.

Our interviews were taped, then edited with the interviewees' cooperation to provide only the comments which we believe will be most helpful to beginning screenwriters.

ERNEST LEHMAN
Screenwriter-Producer-Director

Ernest Lehman, following his graduation from the College of the City of New York, was a copy editor of a Wall Street financial publication, and later a successful freelance writer of magazine articles. He wrote more that fifty stories and novelettes which were published in leading magazines. Two of the novelettes, "The Comedian" and "Sweet Smell of Success," later appeared in book form. "The Comedian" appeared on *Playhouse 90* and won an Emmy; "Sweet Smell of Success" became a memorable movie. Lehman began his award-winning screenwriting career at Paramount with the film *Executive Suite*.

His screenplays include: *Sabrina, The King and I, Somebody Up There Likes Me, Sweet Smell of Success* with Clifford Odets, *North by Northwest, From the Terrace, West Side Story, The Prize, The Sound of Music, Who's Afraid of Virginia Woolf? Hello, Dolly! Portnoy's Complaint,* and *Family Plot.*

My advice to screenwriters is: Be very lucky. It seems to me that as much hard work goes into the writing of a bad film as a good one. So many things determine the quality of what is finally on the screen. Most important is the screenplay, but there's a lot that can happen to it along the way.

Many things can cause a movie to go wrong—how the picture is cast, who directs it, *how* he directs it, what problems arise during the shooting of the film. If you are going to adapt something to the screen, you have to be damn sure that the material you choose is dramatizable. There are some works which achieve great popularity, both books and plays, which resist adaptation to the screen. It is particularly difficult to do a good movie based on a play, because plays are usually written for only one or two sets. However, there are some free-wheeling plays, especially off-Broadway productions, that aren't one-set plays at all.

I don't mean to say that there have never been good movies based on plays. One that comes to mind is *Watch on the Rhine* by Lillian Hellman. I saw the play and the movie, and they were both very, very moving. *The Little Foxes* was done as a movie and was an artistic though not a commercial success.

Writers often wonder if there is such a thing as a good or a bad title for a movie. I don't think there's such a thing as a bad title, if you mean one that will affect its box office appeal. *Dog Day After-noon* was not a good title. *One Flew Over the Cuckoo's Nest* is not a good title. But the minute the film is a success, as these were, the title becomes a good title. *Death of a Salesman* wasn't a good title for a play until the play opened and was a smash. If the title comes from a best-seller, it automatically builds interest in the movie.

I can't give much advice on how to set about writing an original screenplay. Marketing it in today's market is totally different from the way it used to be. Solutions to the writing problems—what to bear in mind when one writes a movie, what makes it good and what makes it mediocre (as though any of us really knows)—depend largely upon the writer's instinctive understanding of his craft. There are no real rules. I can spot a poor screenplay the minute that I start reading, or during the first moments of viewing the movie. But when I'm writing one, I'm not that smart. I hardly ever know if it is good or bad when I'm working on it.

I used to write short stories and articles before I came to Holly-wood and became a film writer. I always believed in hooking the reader as fast as possible and never letting him off the hook, the theory being that the minute you relax and let a reader get a little bored you may lose him. I've maybe overdone that a little in my movies, but that's my particular bag as a writer. I'm always afraid of losing the audience. There are quite a few film makers who share that view, but they are not always necessarily the best. There are some writers and directors who do things at their own leisurely pace, and somehow their own art gradually evolves.

I may be excessively concerned with wanting the audience to become interested quickly, and to get into the dramatic situation early on. I want the audience to be sufficiently hooked and led on so that they are constantly in a state of anticipation. I don't want them to feel that they can go out to the candy counter for five minutes and not have missed anything. I don't want them to leave or talk or do anything but look at that screen. But there are some really incredibly gifted film makers like Stanley Kubrick who have a totally different approach. In his movie *2001—A Space Odyssey,* there were long stretches in which he obviously didn't say to himself, "Oh, God, I'd better not do this, this lasts twenty minutes! How can I keep an audience sitting there for all that time when nothing is happening really in terms of story or narrative or suspense or emotional portrayals?" But he did it, and the overall effect was incredible.

I really believe that pictures should tell a story. That's their number-one function. I believe they should be relatively free of obscurity. Some films are too fuzzy and esoteric for my tastes, though they are often quite artistic. In a movie I always like to know what the hell is going on, what the characters are thinking and feeling at any given moment. I don't like to be given options, the opportunity to wonder "Was he pleased to hear that news?" or "Was he upset by that news?" I want it written, directed, and acted so that I know exactly what is intended. In other words, clarity. That is the best kind of screenwriting. Clarity! People say, "Don't write too much so that it becomes obvious." But there's a fine line between being too obvious and being so afraid of being obvious that you get obscure and nobody knows what you are intending.

Writers need to understand how important the first ten minutes of a movie are. I'm just saying ten minutes arbitrarily; some people might say fifteen or nine or twenty. I stick with ten minutes at the most. People come to a movie and will put up with almost anything for about ten minutes. So you don't have to hook them the very first minute or two. Still, if it's at all possible, I like to make it within the first ten minutes. No more.

In a movie you've got a captive audience, to some extent. They start resenting it when they begin shifting in their seats and thinking, "God, when is something going to *happen?*" They'll give you about ten minutes. That's a good piece of advice for screenwriters to remember.

When I am writing a screenplay I always bear in mind, consciously or unconsciously, that someone is going to read the script, and it has to appeal to that person, whether it be the producer, the director, an actor we're trying to sign, or the head of the studio.

My main concern is that it has to work as a movie, but in the writing of it I make sure that it *reads* well, that it's easy to follow. I've read many screenplays. I don't know whether they were ever made as films, but some of them were written in such manner that the reader would have a lot of trouble following them. The writers were too concerned with breaking down every little thing into a shot, there were never any master scenes, and the narrative sections were not interesting.

This bit of advice may be obvious: read as many screenplays as you can get your hands on, particularly those that became films which you have seen or can see. You can usually get them from state universities or colleges, many of which have film libraries ranging from adequate to excellent. There is no better way to learn how to write a screenplay. I don't mean to put down cinema courses in schools, because I've never been to one. But if somebody asks me how I learned how to do it I say, "I was a movie fan. I went to the movies all my life. I know what movies are. They are a flow of scenes, those scenes have to have motion and conflict, and they shouldn't be up there on the screen too long, and they should move *forward* and carry the story forward, and that's how you write movies."

There are specific mechanical aids I have used that might be helpful to others. I have written outlines of scenes on index cards and put them on a corkboard. Looking at the cards, I could see that I had, say, twenty-eight of them for act 1, only seven for act 2, and twelve for act 3. It was clear that act 1 was much too long, or that shots from it needed to be moved over, or that others needed to be eliminated. I was able to step back and look at the whole picture, in a sense.

But, mind you, if I use a total of forty-two cards, that doesn't necessarily mean that the script will be forty-two times as long as one card. One card may just represent a little bit of a scene, and another card may represent an eight-page scene. But when you look at the cards you sense all that.

I think another bit of advice I would give, whether it's needed or not, is: be aware of the difficulties of conveying exposition. Try to spoon-feed the exposition in such a way that it is palatable, that it doesn't *seem* to be exposition. Try to work it into a scene that has a little bit of conflict so that the character seems to be *forced* to say what he's saying, rather than conveniently saying it to achieve the writer's ends.

My first bit of advice to a writer concerning agents is to try to find one with plenty of clout. I don't sign with an agent for longer than a year at a time. They try to get people to sign for seven years, five years, three years. I sign for a year so there is always a certain amount of pressure on the agent to make me happy because it's always coming up time for the agency contracts to be renewed.

Contracts on deals for actors, directors, writers, everyone, come from the big legal departments of the various studios. What they usually get is a deal memo from an executive at the studio saying, "We have just concluded a deal with so-and-so for his services in writing a screenplay on the following terms. . . . Please draw up the papers and send them to the agency that represents him." There are a million things that are not covered in those negotiations, you know. There are some things that are covered, like money, the time period, the percentage of participation, if any, the billing size and advertising on the screen, and so on.

Now you, the writer, start working. You are writing an original screenplay for x number of dollars for the first draft, plus x more dollars upon completing the final revision. You start working, and you're into the project for weeks or even months. Then along come the contracts, and your agent calls and says, "Look, we've got the contracts but there are about twenty-eight points that we have to talk about. It's not right."

The studio executive is called in. He says, "I never agreed to so-and-so." The writer's agent says, "Oh, but you did." You realize that you have been working for several weeks, maybe months, and they are still negotiating your contract. I've learned to insist that after a deal is closed verbally, a deal memo has to be drawn, a short form letter which is signed by the agent and by the studio executive who made the deal. It has to reflect the salient points of the agreement, and it is signed by both parties. In a sense, it is a short-form contract while I'm waiting for the long form to come. This is a very good thing for beginning screenwriters to keep in mind.

A writer should never sign an open-end deal. Let's say that Joe Smith has written an original screenplay. Now he is marketing it or his agent is trying to market it for him. He is selling a property, so he has to work out the billing and the percentage of participation, if any. He needs to know if he has to provide any revisions if they are wanted. Maybe they'll say, "We'll pay x dollars and this percentage of the profits, but for that you have to agree to do at least ten weeks of revisions." Some determination should be made as to exactly how many weeks of revisions will be needed. A maximum must be stipulated and made part of the deal. The writer usually should request that if further revisions are needed, beyond the ten weeks specified, they will have to pay him x dollars per week. He will agree to make every reasonable attempt to keep himself available but he is definitely on a non-exclusive basis at that point. If he's around or available to do those revisions after the ten weeks, he'll do them. But if he's off in China or someplace working on another film, or if he simply doesn't want to do it, they can't make him do it.

A writer may not want to work on further revisions, simply because he's sick and tired of rewriting. Maybe he hates the director. Maybe he thinks the whole picture has been screwed up. Maybe he has compromised so often in the revisions he has been asked to do that he can't wait to get away from the picture.

Many times screenwriters don't have good communication with the director. Directors sometimes wish screenwriters would disappear from the face of the earth the moment the script is finished. They don't like even to acknowledge that the writer exists. So the screenplay had better communicate to the director what the writer had in mind, or the writer is never going to get it up there on the screen.

In my own writing I use a lot of camera directions, but I know that that can be mere eyewash. It all depends on who the director is, and whether or not he wants that kind of writing. But half the time the writer will not know who the director is going to be. I find it pretty hard not to put a lot of visuals into screenplays. It seems kind of ridiculous not to, if you have an idea how you would like to see something shot. I say, put it all in. The worst that can happen is that the director thinks it is a terrible idea. But at least you put it in there.

There are some directors who are more interested in my "directorial" ideas than others. Like Robert Wise, who has directed four pictures I wrote. The first one was *Executive Suite,* the others were *Somebody Up There Likes Me, West Side Story,* and *The Sound of Music.*

I wrote the whole opening sequence of *The Sound of Music* while I was sitting in my office with my eyes closed. I made believe I was floating over the Austrian Alps and saw specifically what I wanted to see on the screen and what feeling I wanted to get, and wrote it into the screenplay, and that's what I got on the screen. That is, Bob Wise got it on. I spent weeks in Salzburg doing research before writing the screenplay.

One big problem for me was to figure out how we were going to do that long "Do Re Mi" number, which played for eleven and a half minutes on the stage. I had the idea that if I could find places where I could break it without breaking the flow of the song, but cut right on a certain beat of music to another locale, we could also cut through time and have this number geared to show a long period of time in the growing relationship of Maria and the children, rather than its screen limit of eleven and a half minutes. That's the way I did it, and I would say that it was an effective contribution to the picture.

I had to immerse myself in the musical score, of course. In a musical, the numbers are like milestones. They are the plot points you have to get to unless you are going to throw the number out completely.

There is another point I would stress to a beginning screenwriter —the value of rewriting. I would say I write from four to six drafts of each screenplay before the final shooting script.

I usually take my time; I would say four months is a good estimate of how long it would take me to write the first draft. I wrote six drafts of *Who's Afraid of Virginia Woolf?* and on *Black Sunday* I wrote four drafts, though other writers worked on the final shooting script.

I used to take forever to squeeze out a scene. It took me a year to write *North by Northwest,* a year for the first draft, because I would spend hours thinking about it and saying to myself, "It's not good enough."

In conclusion, I would say that that is the very best attitude a writer can take towards his screenplay as he is writing it: "It's not good enough." Perhaps if he thinks that and says it often enough while the movie is still in his typewriter, he'll never think that, and say it, when the picture gets to the screen.

ROBERT EVANS
Producer

Robert Evans was head of World-Wide Production for Paramount Pictures for ten years, the longest tenure of any studio head since 1945. Currently he is an independent producer with Paramount; in this capacity his first production was the award-winning *Chinatown*.

Born in New York City, Evans made his radio acting debut when he was eleven years old and appeared in more than three hundred radio programs. He also appeared on several major TV shows when television was in its infancy. At seventeen, he was the youngest disc jockey with his own radio show in the country, and he became a partner in Evan-Picone, Inc., when he was twenty.

Evans had film roles in *The Man with a Thousand Faces* (in which he portrayed Irving Thalberg, the famous young producer), *The Sun Also Rises, The Fiend Who Walked the West,* and *The Best of Everything.*

As an independent producer at Twentieth Century–Fox, he purchased *The Detective* for filming. Later he became head of production at Paramount Pictures during the period when Paramount produced *The Odd Couple, Romeo and Juliet, Goodbye, Columbus, Rosemary's Baby, Love Story, The Sterile Cuckoo, A New Leaf, Play It Again, Sam, Harold and Maude, The Longest Yard, The Conversation, Save the Tiger, The Great Gatsby, Lady Sings the Blues, True Grit, Paper Moon, Murder on the Orient Express, The Godfather,* and *The Godfather, Part II.*

The one title "producer" has more ambiguity than any other creative name above the film title. Everyone knows what a writer is, everyone knows what a director is, everyone knows what a cinematographer is; but the word "producer" fits many forms. There are packagers, there are agents, there are promoters, there are financiers, and there are producers. And the reason for the ambiguity as to what a producer is, is because in every picture a producer fits a different structure. Every picture a director directs, a writer writes, but a producer does not necessarily produce. Many producers are packagers, or lawyers, or money men.

Many producers are involved with up to six to ten pictures a year. In actuality, one cannot creatively produce this quantity of film and have the involvement that would constitute calling him the producer. I think a better word, and I say it respectfully, would be a "presenter."

The other end of the pendulum is a Sam Spiegel who will do a picture once every five years, be involved with every word that is said in the script, be involved with everyone hired on the picture, and devote his entire efforts to every minute detail.

If I were to look at myself, I tend to be closer to a Spiegel than a Salkind. While I do not wish to make one picture every five years, I also do not wish to make five pictures every year. Making one film to me is a full-time obsession.

I think there are a thousand nuances that go into a film, and I want to be involved with every one of them; I like the minutiae.

The four elements that constitute the anatomy of a film are pre-production, production, post-production, and marketing. And, for better or worse, I am intricately involved in all four elements.

There is also a fifth element, the foreign versions of your English-speaking pictures. A film is re-scripted, re-dubbed, and re-acted in four languages—French, Italian, German, and Spanish. Each of these versions has to be totally supervised from a creative standpoint to achieve the quality that your film has in the English language. How many times have we seen an Italian or French picture in the English dubbed version and, in seeing it dubbed, the film is totally ruined.

Without close supervision that is what can happen to our films. A producer who is really a producer is usually on the film longer than anyone else. He hires everyone including the director and should be involved with the film throughout play dates around the world. That's what a producer's function should be. And the problem is there are very few producers today who do that.

There are a lot of promoters, a lot of agents; there are a lot of packagers, but very few producers. A packager gets a script, finds a director who wants to do it, two stars who want to be in it, and it's sold to a studio as a package.

As this is for the writer's handbook, I can say I would rather have the next five commitments of Robert Towne than Robert Redford. I believe the most important element in any film is the script, and if I get a Robert Towne screenplay every top actor will want to read it. In actuality the script is your biggest star, and the mistake too many of us make is covering up inferior material with star names. When one builds a home, if the structure doesn't hold, no matter how well you paint the rooms, the house falls apart. It is no different in films.

If I were running a studio again I think I would sign fifty writers and that's all. I'd have six people working for me finding writers and interesting screenplays for that is the magnet to attract every other element of talent. Your actors are usually interested in the director. Your director is only interested in the property. Your producer is the one who should find the properties. It doesn't matter who stars in it, the mainstay of any successful picture is the quality of the script.

In the films I wish to make my preference always leans toward people stories. To me, if the characters aren't there, if the people aren't there—I don't care how big the canvas is—it won't be interesting. You can have 10,000 soldiers in the field and not have any feeling for them. You can have two people in a room and be totally involved. *Love Story* is a good example. The reason *The Godfather* works well is you're interested in the people. There had never been a successful Mafia picture before because the people were tinsel, they weren't real. Mario Puzo made those people real. Even though they killed people, you were involved with them and you cared for them. That's a difficult part of writing.

Writers aren't writing women's roles. The reason they are not writing them is that it's easy writing roles for men. Men have a lot of props. For a man you can write guns, horses, gambling, racing with cars. But a woman doesn't have these. The one thing a woman has is mystery, and that's much more difficult to write. Women have been written badly these last decades. They've been written as a tapestry—there is no texture.

I believe there is a great audience desire for men-women stories, not necessarily women stories, but men-women stories. Getting a good love story today seems almost impossible. One of the reasons is that it is difficult to express what love is because the mores have changed so much in the last twenty years. For some reason, the more sexual movies become, the less romantic they are; and maybe I am a romantic, but in the years to come, I believe romance will become more fashionable.

It's my belief that women are hungry for relationship stories and that's why I always try to make women roles in my movies important and not just tapestry.

In *Marathon Man* the girl's part is very important because she is the catalyst and has great mystery. In *Black Sunday* I would have to say that the woman's role is the lead part in the picture and is equal in importance to the two men's roles.

Very few good roles have been written for women because it takes more time and thought, as writing mystery takes more time than writing action.

Speaking of interesting women's roles, Bob Towne gave me a one-line idea that became *Chinatown.* We were sitting at Dominic's restaurant one evening and he said, "I have an idea about a detective told in the thirties when L.A. was a small town; he gets involved with a case, and the case he's involved with has nothing to do with what he's really involved with. The real problem is a woman whom he does not understand." And from that one-line idea, eighteen months later we had a script. It's a beautifully done screenplay that took a lot of work. To do an original can be very painstaking. Bob had a lot of problems in writing it. But he won the Academy Award for it.

Bob Towne to me is what I really consider an honorable, as well as brilliant, screenwriter. By honorable—he doesn't look for the assignment, he'll take the time, he doesn't care. We gave him very little money for *Chinatown*—twenty-five thousand dollars to do it, against a large amount if the picture were made. But he believed in it; he worked on this for eighteen months for only $25,000.

You asked about budget. If you want to make a picture you can find a way to make it. It can be rewritten. It *can* be done. If I like something and I want to do it, I don't worry about the cost of the film. You can be inventive and change things to make it work.

Financing comes from many sections. I'm under the umbrella of Paramount Pictures, and they do the total financing. If I were not, I could get financing. There are many sources of financing films today. It is not difficult to get films made if you have the right elements. But I'll give you the bad news. Because pictures cost so much to make, both the below-the-line costs and the-above-the-line —meaning the writer, the director, the producer, and the actor— have gotten so high that fewer films are being made. Financiers are more name-conscious than ever before because of that.

There is always the big spender coming to town who pays these astronomical amounts of money and it puts everything else out of kilter. I think it hurts our business terribly. As an example, let's take a major film company. It is given a budget by its board of directors of $30 million a year. Now, it used to be that when the average film cost three and four million that they could make ten or twelve pictures. But now the average film is six or seven million, and there are just fewer pictures being made. And if there are fewer pictures made, there are less people getting work, there are less opportunities being given for new people, and those fewer pictures are going to be made by the same people.

I have a few things in development. At the moment I have an original love story that I am having written; the title is *I Love You*. I hope this is my next project, followed by two Robert Towne screenplays, *White Dog*, based on a Romain Gary novel, and *The Two Jakes*, which is a continuation of the J. J. Gittes character of *Chinatown* ten years later.

I also have a book that I'm working with the author on, and if I'm pleased with the manuscript I'll go to the screenplay. It was a thirty-page treatment, and I thought it was a marvelous idea for both a novel and a screenplay.

There are many ways of nurturing along a project. As an example, Mario Puzo's book *The Godfather* was originally presented as a thirty-page treatment and he needed $5,000 up front to pay bills (to him that seemed a lot), then another $5,000, and another $5,000, and another $5,000. We only put up $25,000 against $75,000. We owned the property for really very little money, but he became a very rich man as a result of our agreement. That's as it should be. And he well deserved it.

No matter how good your property is, as a writer, if it's not handled under the right auspices, it can get lost. That is unfortunate, but that's the way it is in films. As an example, when I was head of the studio and an original script went to the readers, even if they had given it a good report, I still wouldn't have received it. However, that very script—if it were presented to me by a director I wanted to work with, or an actor who had read it, or a producer whom I had respect for—then I would certainly read it.

I get scripts sent to me all the time that they don't even accept here because of plagiarism problems.

I don't have time to read 100 scripts a week nor do the directors. They'd never have time to direct a picture—they'd be reading scripts all week. Unless I have a script presented to me under auspices of some regard, I don't even read it. I have on an average of twenty to forty scripts a week that come here. I'm not going to read them unless I get a call from a specific agent or a director or a very close friend who says, "I know you're looking for something like this. I think you should look at it." And then I'll give it to my reader to look at. If it's of interest, then I'll read it. It's difficult for the writer. If a writer has a property—whether it's an idea, a treatment, a screenplay, a novel—it should be presented under some professional auspices; otherwise it will get lost and that can be terribly frustrating to the writer.

Now as far as a studio is concerned, they have to make a certain amount of pictures a year and are looking for all kinds of subject matter. Scripts go to the literary department and they give it to various producers. It depends how important the material is. If it's written by Leon Uris and it's a new book, it's going to be read by the principles in the company. But in presenting it to the studio it still has to be presented professionally.

Looking for Mr. Goodbar was bought by Paramount last year. Eighteen months ago, they read the book and bought it from the galleys. They bought the property, they owned it themselves, and then they made a deal with a producer.

Black Sunday was owned by the studio and they gave it to me because I was interested in doing it. It was that simple. *Marathon Man* was different—I was head of the studio at the time I bought it from the galleys for my own company. I wanted to make it.

I would say the industry is going in the direction of the writer. Because you realize more and more that no matter how big the star is in the picture, if the story isn't any good the picture will not be successful. And I really believe the biggest star in this industry is the writer. I feel very strongly about that. I've given many interviews out to the press, on television, to colleges, to Brown University where I'm an adjunct professor, and my line is I'd rather have the next five commitments of Robert Towne than the next five commitments of Robert Redford. In speaking to young filmmakers, the one thing I stress is that your script and your story are your biggest stars.

DELBERT MANN
Director-Producer

Delbert Mann was graduated from Vanderbilt University and did postgraduate work at the Yale School of Drama. A B-24 pilot in World War II, he was awarded the Distinguished Flying Cross with four oak leaf clusters after thirty-five European missions. He is past president of the Directors' Guild of America.

His TV experience began in 1949 as an assistant director. He was promoted shortly to director of the *Philco TV Playhouse*, associated with producer Fred Coe. The next six years saw him direct more than one hundred live TV shows, including Paddy Chayefsky's *Marty, Bachelor Party*, and *Middle of the Night*. His other TV productions include *What Makes Sammy Run, Darkness at Noon, The Day Lincoln Was Shot, Yellow Jack*, and *The Petrified Forest;* productions for *Omnibus, Playhouse 90, Ford Jubilee, Lights Out*, and *Playwrights '56;* and the musical *Our Town*, starring Frank Sinatra, and *The Plot to Kill Stalin*, Look Award Winner of 1958.

Mann was named one of "Filmdom's Famous Five" directors by the trade publication *Film Daily*, in both 1955 and 1962, and his direction of *Lover Come Back* and *That Touch of Mink* earned him the title of "Top Money-making Director of 1962."

Motion pictures: *Marty, The Bachelor Party, Desire Under the Elms, Separate Tables, Middle of the Night, The Dark at the Top of the Stairs, The Outsider, Lover Come Back, That Touch of Mink, A Gathering of Eagles, Dear Heart, Mister Buddwing, Kidnapped*, and *Birch Interval*.

Recent television specials: *Heidi, David Copperfield, Jane Eyre, The Man Without a Country, The First Woman President, A Girl Named Sooner, The Francis Gary Powers Story*, and *After He's Gone*.

The producer is the executive responsible to the money people and to the studio for bringing all the major elements of the package together, including the story idea, the screenwriter, the director, the major cast, and the budget. The director is the man who is actually charged with and responsible for the doing of the show. So it's easy to see that the two jobs frequently overlap and intertwine and are often handled by one person.

Many directors prefer serving as their own producer because of the additional authority it gives them over all elements of the production. But there are many of the producer's duties which I don't particularly care for.

For instance, a good producer takes ultimate responsibility for the picture in terms of its marketing, its final distribution, and its advertising. The producer with whom I recently worked, Robert Radnitz, is outstanding in that respect. He follows his individual pictures through to the very end, travels to various cities around the country, and promotes and promotes, feeling that this is a large part of his responsibility as a producer. That's an aspect of the job which I don't care for at all.

Yet it must be done. Particularly in today's independent world where the major studios no longer operate as they did twenty or thirty years ago. Maybe you could draw a rough parallel between the commander in chief of a naval fleet and the captain of the ship. The producer is in general charge of all the ships in the flotilla—or all the elements of a film from budget to distribution. The director is the man who is directly responsible for the safety and conduct of a single ship—the film itself. He works with and, in a sense, under the admiral, under the producer. Yet he is the man who has to have the ultimate authority over all aspects of the actual production. The two of them must see eye to eye or the project can be in serious trouble. The casting, from star down to every minor part, is the director's responsibility. However, the producer also has ultimate responsibility for obtaining the major stars who are necessary to attract the money to finance the film.

When it comes to putting the script on film, setting up the scenes, rehearsing the actors, working with the costumers, the prop men, the art director, the location manager, the cameramen, all those things are the director's responsibility. Somebody has to have charge of the ship, and in terms of operations the director is the man responsible.

The director is responsible for the progress of the film, keeping on schedule or close to schedule, keeping on budget or close to budget. He is responsible for the staging and look of every scene and every shot. He is the one who works with the cameraman and to whom the cameraman is responsible for the lighting of every scene, the mood of it, the style of it, the look and feel of it. The art director is responsible to the director. The actors are directly responsible to the director—and the director to them. That's a one-to-one relationship for which the director has the final responsibility. He is the one who works with the actors and with these key technical people on his set to shoot the scenes, to get the film put together. Then he works with the editor in the editing and putting it all together. The producer is also concerned with the final editing, so once again, it is hopefully a cooperative effort between producer and director.

The director and producer's co-responsibilities continue through the post-production stage. This includes the final process of dubbing sound, of mixing the sound, of looping the lines that need to be repaired, of working with the composer to place the music and to score the music, to see that it is put in properly, to work with the laboratory to get the final kind of look and print that is wanted.

I understand why many writers are disturbed to keep hearing that film is a director's medium, and why they are disturbed because control of the project does get out of their hands. While they have created a script alone, or have worked on it with a producer or a director, the actual visualizing of it or putting it on film gets totally away from them. It becomes the director's responsibility, and the film becomes the director's vision of what it should be. If the writer is lucky and has written a good script, this may result in the director's vision closely corresponding with his own. Or it may turn out to be a total change from the writer's point of view. It may be a total distortion, or it may be a total improvement. But it does get away from him, and the control goes over to the director.

Somebody has to be in charge of the vision of the picture. When you are shooting a picture, perhaps totally out of continuity, the actors have to depend on the director for the emotional line of the piece. They may shoot the last scene first, they may shoot the middle next, they may shoot the first scene last. Somebody has to have the total vision—to string all scenes together in the proper tempo, the proper rhythm, the proper emotional ups and downs, the proper nuances and subtleties of playing. That can only be one person. It can't be done by committee. That man is the director.

In the theater the writer is present throughout all of the rehearsals and has a much stronger voice in what script changes are made. The writer has the time, the authority, and the commitment to be there, and to make the rewrites which prove to be necessary. The mechanics of film are so different from theater that the writer is, almost without exception, prevented from a day-to-day participation in film making.

It is true that many directors prefer not to have the writer on the set. That depends on the relationship between the two. I have had a few experiences where I would prefer not to have the writer present, where I felt I must have total freedom to make the changes as the actors and I work them out together when we are in the process of shooting. On the other hand, my training in live television taught me to work with the writers in a kind of theater-type situation. This means a rehearsal period with the writer there to make the changes necessary. It is one thing to sit in a room with a typewriter and envision a scene. It is quite another thing when actors perform that scene. Sometimes it simply won't play. Somebody has to change it. Therefore, writers and directors in live television practice the theater method of working together, and it worked beautifully for all of us.

I generally welcome the opportunity to have a writer with me throughout. He is one to whom I can turn and confer in the process of working with the actors, in the process of getting a scene to play properly. I can say, "Look, it's not working. Something is wrong in that beat. Something has to be changed. What is it?" Then we can work it out together. It is a luxury to have the writer there to say, "Yes, I see what you mean. Give me a few minutes." It's a marvelous way to work.

In the beginning, in order to acquaint myself with the writer's vision of the film, I read a script to see what it tells me, whether it interests me, whether it moves me. I read it just for content as one would read any novel. It's important to block out enough time so it can be read from beginning to end without a lot of interruptions. This is the only way you can get the whole flow of the piece. If I find that the script is something that interests me, something I want to do, then I start to reread, reread, reread. I try to become absorbed in what the writer is trying to say. I find out where I think he has failed, where I think he has succeeded. The director's job, like the actor's, is an interpretive one. This is predicated, of course, upon the premise that it is already a fully completed script.

In many, many instances, more often on feature films than in television, the director (and/or the producer) works with the writer from the very inception of the project. This means numerous story conferences during which they work out the project together.

As an example, I've just finished nine months of work with a writer on a screenplay. Together we worked on six rewrites of a very complicated, very expensive screenplay. I became involved in the project when it was in the roughest kind of brief outline form. The writer and I conferred many times before he ever wrote the first draft. We were brought together by a producer who believed in the project and was putting up the money for both of us.

Beginning writers often ask me if it is permissible or desirable for them to specify their choice of directors when they submit their scripts to studios or producers. I tell them that is their option. In a sense, a writer is "casting" his film by thinking in terms of a director who will be sensitive to it or actors who are right for it, and he certainly should have the right to make such suggestions.

Young writers are concerned about how long their scripts should be. If it's for television the script should be reasonably close to its intended length, from 100 to 120 pages for a two-hour production. An average feature film should probably be in the area of 120 pages unless it's a spectacle. Obviously there have been plenty of films shot at 150 pages or more. Or far less. There is no rule. It depends so much on intangibles. If it's a small, personal, intimate story, it simply will not stand being done at 150 pages; the audience will go to sleep on you. If it's an action story, a war story for instance, it could very well be 150 pages and still move very quickly.

I never try to discourage writers from writing fully at first, however. I ask them to put it all down the way they feel it. Maybe it comes in at 170 pages, and that may be the best way to start. Such a script may include a lot of things that are never going to get on film, but it does tell the director more about what the writer has in mind.

This doesn't always hold true for television scripts, where, because of the pressures of limited time and money, there is a necessity to move quickly. Normally in feature films you have a little bit more luxury in terms of time and budget. Nevertheless, I find that in examining my own attitudes toward work that I tend to encourage writers to write fully, to put it all down. But that doesn't mean that I'm going to follow it in every detail.

Camera directions give me a picture of what the writer has in mind. For instance, the writer may suggest a close angle shot in a particular scene. I may say, "No, I want to be somewhere else entirely with the camera at that time, the actors are doing something entirely different." Still, I try to remain faithful to the writer's version of his material.

Just because it's in the script and because I encourage the writer to write so that he expresses to me what he sees doesn't mean that I'm duty bound to accept that or do it his way. I just take that as added input from the writer, and it helps create an image for me. If I feel that it is wrong or at variance from the values I see, I feel no reservations about doing it quite differently.

At the same time, I thoroughly enjoy working with a creative writer. It is marvelous when we can talk out these problems together. I try to put his work on the screen the best I can to interpret what he has written. That is my job. But I can't just follow slavishly. If I do that, then he is the director and he should be the one who is held responsible for the final results.

If a scene is not right I may have to rewrite it myself if he is unavailable. Even in feature pictures where you are not faced with a finite limit of time, you try to get rid of extra pages. It is your responsibility to keep the costs within the budget and to keep on schedule.

I appreciate beautiful descriptive prose in a script, but when I come to preparing it to go into production, for the cameraman to read, for the art director to read, for the prop man to read, and for the actors to read when I'm casting, I try to have that script just as lean and tight as possible. It's a much more realistic way of scheduling and budgeting. It enables you to know much more about such things as what set you're going to be shooting on a given day and how long your actor is going to be tied up. If you get sloppy in that area and allow a lot of things to slide through that you're not sure are ever going to get on the screen, you will suddenly find that you are three million dollars over budget and six weeks over schedule and you're down the drain.

Scripts come to me from every source possible—through my agent, through a producer, from a network, a studio, from a writer, or from material that I have searched out myself.

I think it's necessary to read as many scripts as I can. It's very hard to keep up with all that I receive, and often I have to tell a writer that it may be months before I will have a chance to read his script.

I enjoy working with any well-written script, but I must confess that for me comedy is the hardest thing to do. I like comedy. It's fun. But at the end of a day when I am doing a comedy I go home really exhausted. I think it's primarily because of the number of choices available as to how far to go, where the right single thing is that will generate a laugh, or how to build to the next laugh, which may lie on the next page. The subtlety of comedy timing and playing is difficult. I enjoy it and think I do it reasonably well, but to know in advance which precise value is going to provide the biggest laugh is a very, very tough job. But I do find that when I read a script and it makes me laugh out loud, and occasionally one will do that, I can be sure it's a pretty darn good script.

FRANK ROSENFELT
President, Metro-Goldwyn-Mayer

Frank Rosenfelt is a graduate of Cornell University and Cornell Law School. He served in the United States Army, 1943–46. In 1955 he joined the MGM legal department, was elected vice-president and general counsel in 1969, became president in 1973, and was elected chief executive officer in 1974.

In making a motion picture the studio generally finances the film and distributes or supervises the distribution of it. If it's financing the film, it reviews or supervises the making of the picture in every stage of its production.

Motion pictures, like any other piece of merchandise, must be distributed properly. You can manufacture the finest automobile in the world, but if the public doesn't know about it and doesn't know where to buy it or if it has to go to too much trouble to buy it, it won't sell. The same thing is true of a motion picture. A distributor normally charges approximately 30 percent, or 30 cents of every dollar, to cover his overhead costs in distribution. The overhead costs include a substantial sales force in the United States alone; there are thirty branches on which he's paying for the lights, the rent, taxes and so on, various secretaries and other personnel. What that costs in terms of the films that are distributed by a company each year really depends upon how many pictures they distribute.

Let's assume that all of that machinery is used to distribute one picture and that picture grossed $10 million (by "gross" I mean dollars that the distributor gets, not the box office). But suppose his fixed cost is $4 million. That would mean that the cost of distribution, forgetting about advertising and prints, is obviously 40 percent. If he's charging only 30 percent, he's losing money on distribution. If the distributor has two pictures and, instead of $10 million, they bring in $20 million, obviously the overhead cost per picture then for distribution, instead of being 40 percent is 20 percent, and though he is charging 30 percent he hasn't gone into the black yet. Let me clarify this. He has also laid out millions of dollars for prints, advertising, and other items of distribution—shipping expenses and so on. He hasn't got that back yet. He has financed the picture to the extent of x millions, he hasn't got that back yet, so until he gets all of that money back you can't say that he's broken even. And most pictures do not break even. People continue making films because the highs —when a film does hit, it can be very profitable—can make up for an awful lot of the loss on marginal films.

Distributors do invest in the initial financing of a film more often than not. That is, the distributor may buy the book or script on his own initiative or may purchase such a work when it is brought to the studio's attention by a producer.

The film business is a very, very difficult business. And in financial terms it is known as a cyclical business, and that's why there are companies that are on top for a couple of years and are in the depths of depression a few years later when picture after picture loses money. They are about to go into bankruptcy and then they hit a movie like *Jaws* and are on top of the world again.

American Grafitti is a good example. That represented an investment of under a million dollars that returned in this country alone approximately $40 million. Now that's not $40 million profit but, with less than a $1 million negative cost, a substantial portion of it was profit. And you can't do that in the automobile business or manufacturing suits—but you can sleep better manufacturing suits because you know that a suit costs $20 to make and you're selling it for $39.50. You know where your outlets are, how many suits you are going to produce a year, who's going to buy them, and so on. But it isn't as much fun as the film business.

Distribution agreements are fairly standard. They have been worked out over a period of twenty-five years, and a distribution agreement that you make at Fox is not much different from the agreement you will make with Warner's or MGM. But it's not simply distribution that a producer is concerned about. He wants financing as well.

Roughly, here is the procedure: A producer comes in with a script and he says that Arthur Penn has agreed to direct his project and Marlon Brando has agreed to star. It does not make much difference which studio is involved—MGM, Fox, or Universal, etc. The script is read and the head of production at the studio concludes it's a good project for Penn and Brando. He has a budget made up and it indicates that the picture will cost approximately $10 million to produce. Then the sales people make an estimate of the potential worldwide theatrical and television gross of the film. There's a certain amount of educated guesswork involved in this process. If they tell me that, at best, we are going to get back $7 million, my decision is obviously not to make the film. But if it budgets out at a cost of $6 million and my sales people project $20 million in gross film rentals, just as obviously my decision is to go forward.

The producer enters into a contract which provides that the studio will put up all of the money necessary to finance the production of that picture. The contract also generally provides that the studio will own the film, will own the copyright on the film because they paid for it; and the studio will have worldwide distribution rights. It will also provide that the producer will get a producer's fee for his services—for supervising the production—of $75,000 or $100,000 or $150,000, depending on his reputation, experience, and the value of the project. It will provide that the profits derived from the picture will be shared in a certain proportion, so that in addition to his fee there is an opportunity for him to get a percentage of the profits. Although the contract is lengthy and covers a great many details such as representations and warranties, definitions of gross film rentals and net profits, etc., that, basically, is the financing-production-distribution agreement.

The producer then comes here. We provide the studio facilities for him, the stages, and so on, for which he is charged a set rate and for which he pays out of his budget—with our money, so to speak.

The studio will have the right to approve all of the key creative decisions, because it's the studio's money being risked. They will not only approve of the star and the director, they will also approve any of the changes in the script, because changes in the script have a twofold effect: they may result in costs going up or down. Also, so many changes may be made that the studio will conclude, "This isn't the package I bought." So the studio will have control over the various creative elements in the film. That's the way it works.

A company must give consideration to the potential code rating of a film when it begins a project, since the rating can affect the gross potential of the picture. It is a matter of creative ingenuity on the part of the producer and director to make a film which will have an appropriate rating, taking into account the subject matter of the film and the audience it is designed to appeal to. If a film is improperly rated, it can mean the loss of substantial revenue. For example, if a film is rated "R" that was essentially designed as a "PG" film, a substantial portion of the audience, potential customers, will be excluded.

The money-making films are not those that are rated "R." Or those that are rated "PG." They are simply the good, entertaining films, regardless of ratings. When a script is good and I think it is commercially viable, I don't think in terms of whether it is "G," "PG," or "R." However, most companies will look very closely at a film before deciding to be associated with an X-rated film.

The financing of television is a totally different business. The studios finance the development of a potential series. From time to time the network will contribute part of that financing. Then when a series goes on the air, it is licensed for broadcast by one of the three networks. Generally speaking, that network only pays a portion of what it actually costs to produce that particular episode. The license fee may be $250,000 for the hour program and the actual cost to make it will be $285,000, so that the $35,000 is recouped (usually) when it is later syndicated around the country after it has finished its network run, and from foreign sales. First you have to make up your deficit, then, hopefully, there will be a profit.

All scripts sent to MGM by a recognizable agent are read. Unsolicited material is unacceptable primarily for legal reasons. The companies over the years have been involved in needless plagiarism litigation that they can avoid if the scripts come through an established agent; the studio has more confidence when it is dealing with a professional writer. While there always have been plagiarism suits in this industry and I suppose there always will be, no studio will knowingly finance the production of a picture based upon literary material which constitutes an infringement of someone else's material and thereby jeopardize an investment of millions of dollars. Even the threat of potential litigation is regarded as a very serious matter. Let me add, however, that precedent is most important in this area of operation, and for that reason alone a studio will spend large sums of money to fight and win a case that could have been settled for a much lesser amount. Your advice that writers should send a synopsis with their scripts is excellent. Writers have not been doing this, probably because they haven't thought of it. But with so much material to read, it would help our story editors to identify more quickly the subject matter.

At MGM we are constantly looking for the unusual or original in scripts. These days you can see the usual on television.

MICHAEL ZIMRING
Literary Agent

Michael Zimring attended the drama school, Pasadena Playhouse, 1936–37, and was a radio actor in Hollywood and Chicago, 1938–41. He was a captain in the United States Army, 1941–46, heading the theatrical branch of the European Theater of Operations. In 1947 he was assistant to Orson Welles in the Mercury Theatre. Zimring joined the William Morris Agency in 1948 and became the senior agent in the motion picture department in 1950. Since 1959 he has been head of the William Morris literary department.

At its best, the relationship between a writer and an agent is the strongest bond outside of marriage. A good agent makes recommendations, but in the final analysis he carries out the writer's wishes. He never loses sight of the fact that the agent is working for the writer, that the writer is not working for the agent. The agent is in the writer's employ, getting 10 percent of what the writer makes.

Once when I was giving a lecture at UCLA, the first question a young man asked me was, "Do you think you're the best literary agent in the business?" I wasn't prepared for that, but the answer I gave him pretty much expresses my feelings in the matter. "No, I'm not," I said. "There is no best—or worst, either—except in a particular writer's opinion. Every agent in the business is making a living, which proves he is succeeding for somebody. But there isn't an agent in the business who hasn't failed for somebody. I feel sure that every agent has a client who thinks he is the best, but he most likely has also had a client who thinks he was the worst."

It is true that some agents are better than others in that they perhaps succeed more and fail less than some others, but in the final analysis we must not forget that we are in a business of opinions. It is not an absolute business. A hundred people read a script and you may get a hundred different opinions. Who can say which opinion is correct? However, it is my opinion that I must use to decide what I think is salable.

I may tell a writer who has brought a script to me that I just don't feel I'm the right agent to handle it, because I don't feel strongly enough about it, or that I don't think there's a market for it. I always say, "Look, that is my opinion and my opinion only. I'm not saying that what you've written is not good. I'm not a critic, so my opinion in that area is not pertinent. I'm an agent, which means that I'm a salesman, so all I can tell you is whether I think it is salable. And that's not the same thing as saying it's good or not good. Even on the question of its salability, that's still only my opinion. Please try another agent."

I'm sure that there have been properties that I turned down which were later sold by another agent. I know that I have sold scripts which other agents have turned down. We all fail and we all succeed.

It's a devastating thing for a writer to be turned down by anybody. After all, writing is the loneliest business in the world. I know writers who have non-writer collaborators because they need company. They are primarily used as sounding boards.

Writers come in all kinds. Some say they can't write more than three hours a day. Some can write for twenty-four hours, around the clock. I have one such client, an excellent writer. If he had to, he could turn out a screenplay in ten days. He is also a successful novelist, which makes him unusual, because very few writers can do both screenplays and novels well. There was one who wrote a very suspenseful novel which I sold to a major studio. At the novelist's request I made a condition of the deal that he write the screenplay. He wrote the screenplay exactly like the book, but the dialogue that had the reader sitting on the edge of his seat didn't work at all in the screenplay. He just didn't understand that words to be read and words to be spoken have to be written differently. Words that are effective when you read them don't always work when you speak them. They have to be dramatized for the screen.

I usually tell novelists that writing for the screen is the most anonymous form of writing there is. You ask a hundred people on the street who wrote the screenplay based on a successful play or novel and I'll bet you not more than five can tell you. And yet you ask the same hundred who wrote the play or novel and seventy-five or more will know.

The screenwriter gets only money, but the successful novelist or playwright gets fame *and* fortune. Also, the novelist and playwright know that what they write is theirs and cannot be changed. Once a screenplay is written, the writer has lost it. It can be changed and mutilated to the point that he may not even recognize it. And he has no recourse. Some have become so despondent they have tried to remove their name from the credits.

Most of the screenwriting is adapted from other material, but there are screenwriters who write originals for the screen. However, the latter have no more control over what finally appears on the screen than the one who adapts.

The movie business has changed. In the old days we sold everything to the major studios. They put it all together. Everybody was under contract—the writers, directors, producers, and the stars. These people were told which pictures they were to work on and, short of breaking their contracts, they had to do it.

It doesn't work that way now. The major studios have become basically financing and distribution companies, and they don't buy a story or script unless some picture maker in whom they have faith wants to do it. That picture maker is usually a name director. The best way for an agent to place a writer's property is with that picture maker.

When I get a really good script I usually consider first who the best director for that particular screenplay would be. The best way to sell a property is to select the director you think best suited for it and go to him first, advising him you are in effect giving him an exclusive look at it. If he likes it and wants to do it, we—together —go to a major studio or other financing company. In my opinion, the perfect sale is the one that is made to the first and only buyer I go to. In the past we would try to get more than one interest and then try to set up an auction in an effort to get the price as high as possible. Now we know that we can sometimes get an even higher price with that first and only buyer.

It's fine with me if a writer suggests the director he prefers to do his screenplay. Who am I to say no? After all, I *am* working for him.

If a neophyte writer wants a particular agent, he should write to him or phone him. If that fails, keep trying, wheedle the agent's secretary, anything, but keep trying.

The agent cannot afford to sit in an ivory tower. He is nothing if he has nothing to sell. Some people might like to make it sound glamorous, but when you come right down to it an agent is simply a salesman. It's true that we are dealing in a special field, but then most salesmen are.

Writers should call to ask about the progress that is being made on their scripts. The agent may not like being bothered, but a writer can't be concerned about his agent's problems. His only concern is his own problem. The writer should also take advantage of his agent's experience and knowledge of the marketplace at the time he is formulating his idea for an original. I encourage my people to discuss their ideas with me before they start to write. Perhaps he is picking a subject that is just not salable.

As far as agency contracts with writers are concerned, we have a standard agreement. The one thing that may vary is the length of the agreement. The first time a writer is signed, the term is limited to two years. Thereafter, it can be two and a half years. Also, there may be some exclusions in the agreement, such as specific story property that is still covered by a previous agent's agreement or which is otherwise encumbered.

There is also a provision in the agency agreement that an agent must get a writer two weeks' work in a period of ninety days or the writer can discharge him by written agreement.

Writers are always interested, as they should be, in how much money they should expect for an original script. There is no way that you can generalize about the monetary value of an original. There are so many factors involved. The agent is the one who usually determines what the price is going to be. His decision is based on several things—his "feel" for the market, the importance of the subject matter, the budget the eventual picture will have, to name a few. If the dollars are lower than desired, the agent tries to make up for it by getting as great a profit participation as possible.

When I make a film deal for a story property I carefully work out all the details, including separation of rights. Eventually, the lawyers work out the contract itself, but that contract must reflect the deal I have set forth in my booking memorandum. An agent has to know something about law and, after all these years of reading contracts, I sometimes catch things the lawyer missed.

Finally, the selling of a film script depends to a great extent upon proper timing. A subject that couldn't sell a few years ago might be sold today. There might be a novel thirty or forty years old that did not sell at the time it was published because it dealt with a subject that was not acceptable in the film medium. We are more permissive now, so that particular subject can be made today. Also, if an agent has faith in a property he must have the temerity to keep going back to a buyer even after the latter has rejected it. Take the case of *American Graffiti.* That's the second most successful picture Universal ever made, yet it was turned down by every studio in this town, including Universal. Finally, after the third submission, the studio said it would go forward with it on a limited budget if Francis Ford Coppola came in as executive producer on a supervisory basis. They were as surprised as anybody by its enormous success, which proves this is a guessing game. No one can really tell what will captivate the public's attention. And the public's mood constantly changes.

GENE WILDER
Actor-Director-Screenwriter

Gene Wilder attended the University of Iowa and the Old Vic School in England, and has studied with eminent teachers, including Uta Hagen and Lee Strasberg. He has had film roles in *The Adventure of Sherlock Holmes' Smarter Brother* (which he also wrote and directed), *Young Frankenstein* (which he wrote with Mel Brooks), *Blazing Saddles, The Little Prince, Willy Wonka and the Chocolate Factory, Quackser Fortune, Bonnie and Clyde, The Producers, Start the Revolution Without Me, Rhinoceros, Everything You've Always Wanted to Know About Sex, and Silver Streak.*

I always felt a strong awareness—what Lee Strasberg always said was the most important attribute of a director—to be able to sit in the back of the auditorium and say, "What does the audience see at this moment?" And I always felt in screenwriting that I could put myself in the place of an audience and ask what would I want to see next, not what does the writer think would be great. They're sitting there with their boxes of popcorn and I can't explain it to them. There's not going to be any sheets of paper beforehand with a plot summary. What are they going to see that will tell the story? And how boring is it or how interesting is it?

The second film that I wrote was very different from the first one. My third one, which was the first one produced, *Young Frankenstein,* was very different from the first two. I was the principal writer on that film, and then Mel Brooks worked with me on the second, third, and fourth drafts. He taught me that it's not enough to have a script that is good, scene by scene; you have to work on it speech by speech, line by line, word by word. *Sherlock Holmes' Smarter Brother* was my second produced screenplay. I don't plan to make any more parodies on the classics.

More and more I find that an important part of writing is not to do it alone. At least for me. That is, I write alone but I'll talk about a scene that I've written, or an idea for a scene, with friends. Then I listen, listen, listen, and I say, "No, no, no, YES!" Then I rewrite the scene. Talking that way with people with whom you feel comfortable, with whom you can disagree, is important to a writer. Friends who love you and who like your work can give you ideas which you might not like but which can become wonderful if you twist them around and rework them. If you say, "I don't want that," they're not going to cry.

I've never had much difficulty with dialog and never with characters. My only nemesis is plot construction. In my newest one the idea was based on a plot rather than starting with a character, so the plot construction was more or less easy. I have not had difficulty writing. If I have difficulty I won't write. I always say, "Well, I'm not a writer; I'm an actor." So I rip it up and throw it away. It gives me a freedom because if I said that is what I do for my living, this is what God is watching right now, these words, I'd be in a lot of trouble, because every word has to be right and that can freeze you.

I want to please the audience. I want to please the fat lady in Kansas City who sits on her porch swatting flies. I want to please my friends who laugh when I do something funny and who smile politely when it's not so funny as I thought it was. I want to please them. I want to please my mother who is dead—but I don't want to please a producer.

I wrote four drafts of *Sherlock Holmes*. The fifth draft is the shooting script, the sixth draft is the editing script. You change the writing in the editing—you take out a line and put in another one. When you're in the editing room you can see that it's a very talky scene. That's when line cutting is so important.

It takes me about three months to write a draft. Subsequent drafts take about a month each. The second draft is usually a lot of work. The third and fourth drafts are for polishing.

I remember when I wrote my first script, I thought that I should show how well I visualized the scene by saying what the camera was doing. I realized by my third script that nobody gives a damn, least of all the director. In my fourth script, *Sherlock Holmes,* I was directing the film, so I wrote a lot of camera directions as reminders to myself. The big distinction I'm making, and it *is* a big one, is that if a screenwriter asked me, "Should I put in what the camera is doing?" I'd say, "It's an insult to your director."

If you are going to be the director and you don't want to remember every single thing in the form of index cards, notes, letters to an assistant, camera directions are important to help you keep it all focused for four months later when you're shooting that scene. So I'm saying that camera directions depend on whether or not you are directing the film. I would advise screenwriters not to put down camera moves because it only irritates or, at best, causes a lot of work for the director. He wants to add his own dimension to what the author has written, and if he has to follow or wade through everything that the author thought should be happening with the camera, a good director would just cross all of that out and say, "Yes, I understand the intent of your scene, but I'm going to do it the way I visualize your intent. You've intruded onto my area by saying what the camera should be doing." I wouldn't bother about close-ups or inserts or any of those directions unless it's to make the point of a scene. When I put down *close-up* I know that I'm going to be doing a close-up, that it's essential.

I don't recommend using transitions such as dissolve or fade in. When I was editing my first film I realized that they were all changed anyway. Sometimes I found that a fade-out shot would be misleading. Or that it stopped the flow of the picture or it was too abrupt, or whatever. But now when I put it down I do so because I know that it *should* be a fade-out. That little story is done. It doesn't mean I'd be rigid and couldn't change it if the editor had better ideas.

In my new script I have maybe six transitional directions, but I don't have any dissolves and very few cut to's. I do have, I think, four fade-outs because they were little stories that had to end. It has to be at the right time emotionally for the audience, because when you fade out there is a great danger of the audience saying, "Ah, well, that's over, it's the seventh-inning stretch, so I'll get some popcorn." They take it as a cue to relax a little bit. Well, sometimes that's good . . . if you want them to.

My advice to beginning screenwriters about contracts and sales agreements is: Get a good lawyer. Another piece of advice is: Watch out for producers. I think producers should participate in the prof- its of a picture, but I don't think they should participate in the film to the extent that they do. I see a lot of artists being well paid or reasonably well paid and producers getting filthy rich. I'm not against anyone getting rich for having done a lot of work. And I know a lot of producers who have spent a year and a half of their lives on a picture whereas an artist only spent eight weeks or twelve weeks, and I appreciate that distinction. But I also know that there are producers who package films and whose contribution is signifi-

cant only up to a point. I wouldn't compare it with the contribution
of particular artists who I think should share in the profits as much
as the producer. But most producers would go crazy, saying, "What!
Do you mean that I'm only going to get what the composer gets?
Or what the associate producer or the production designer gets, or
the cameraman or the editor?"

I don't describe the physical characteristics of the characters in
my scripts, because there's no point in it. In *Sherlock Holmes* I
already had the three principal parts cast. Why say a character is a
tall man with very thin hair with a little gray at the temples? I can
get a short man or a fat man or a skinny man and I can tell him,
as a director, why the character must have a twitch in his right eye.
He may change that and come up with something better. But there's
no point in saying what the person looks like if you don't know who's
going to play it, and if you do know who's going to play it, the only
reason you'd be putting it down would be for the Library of Congress.

Sometimes I go for clichés in characters and use them for my own
purposes, a tradition from the silent comedies. I like black and white,
sharp red, a giant bald fat man, a thin little wisp of a girl. For
comedy sequences, for really black comedy stuff, it's necessary, I
find, to have those strong contrasts. In that case I would put down
a description.

Always, and consciously, I try to hook the audience in the first
five minutes. I want them right from the start to feel something—
BOOM! I want an explosion right at the beginning. I always want
that.

Truffaut said that he thought that all directors fell into two categories, those who worked to satisfy themselves only and those who
worked to satisfy the audience. Not that they don't overlap, but each
has his primary driving demon force. I suppose I fall into the second
category.

A private piece of beauty, that no one is going to see, and that
doesn't communicate on the screen, is not totally worthless but it is
so special that I don't have any affinity for those kinds of films. It's
not the same as Van Gogh's paintings that were not appreciated at
the time. The nature of film is that it communicates to the people
at the time. For those writers who also want to work the second way,

I would say that the most important faculty they could develop and nourish is the ability to picture themselves in a movie theater, with the lights out, a box of popcorn in their hands, and saying, "Never mind whether I'm writing a masterpiece or not a masterpiece, I'm going to the movies tonight. Would I want to see this?"

Practical Business Advice

Writers are seldom noted for their business acumen, so you will want to become acquainted with the fundamentals needed to cope with the marketplace. First of all you will want to know:

HOW TO MARKET YOUR SCREENWRITING TALENT

You are not only trying to sell scripts, you are trying to sell yourself as a writer of films. Agents are salespeople who need products to sell; in a new writer's script they look beyond that particular submission to the potential apparent in the writing. Your script will show him not only how well you write but how well you understand the demands of the medium. So he looks for two things: first, your writing ability and, second, whether you can be a productive client for him. (Can you handle assignments he gets for you? Will the originality of your concepts find a market in the film industry?)

Don't expect even the most enthusiastic agent to sell the first draft of your screenplay. That would be a phenomenon. But an agent will accept your script—and later, a producer will buy it—on the basis of the talent you have brought to that script and their belief in your ability to rework it into something filmable.

Television is a bottomless maw where film scripts are concerned.

It devours scripts of all kinds—two-hour movies, ninety-minute movies of the week, situation comedies, series based on detectives, cops, doctors, newspapermen, etc., or science fiction, westerns, and the new mini-series which are really novels for television.

The television producer Aaron Spelling is quoted in *The Television Writer's Handbook* by Constance Nash and Virginia Oakey (New York: Harper & Row, 1978) as saying that there is a scarcity of writers in Hollywood. Tony Ford, agent, says, "We're always looking for the new Abby Mann to walk into our office."

These comments should offer real encouragement to serious new screenwriters. Even if your first choice is writing for the movies, getting television credits is an excellent way to break ground. Also, the two-hour movies for television are not substantially different from those for the big screen, so you have two chances at a market.

Agents are not only important to you as salespeople, they will lead you safely through the labyrinth of legalities which are the inevitable consequences of becoming a screenwriter. A close working relationship with your agent will be invaluable to you in many other ways, too, since he is in touch with the current markets and can advise you on which kinds of screenplays are being bought, which kinds are being sought.

Now we arrive at the vicious circle which in the past has stymied beginning writers: in order to sell your script it must be submitted through an agent . . . in order to get an agent you must have sold a script. But how can you sell a script until you have an agent? Take heart. There are now ways to break that circle.

HOW TO GET AN AGENT

First, write a letter to an agent. A list is included in this chapter. Include professional facts about yourself that would interest him in you as a writer, and a description of your works, whether completed or in the making. This letter should be brief but meaty. With your letter send a completed script (or scripts, preferably) with a synopsis attached. The synopsis should not exceed two pages. Make multiple submissions; it is accepted practice to make at least six copies and send them simultaneously. Don't fold your scripts; mail them flat in a manila envelope with a cardboard inserted against the back of the script. If they are too bulky for that, mail them in a padded shipping bag, which you can buy in any stationery store.

Don't expect an answer by return mail. Agents are inundated with scripts from clients and potential clients. They can read only so many scripts at night and on weekends. But remember: They are salespeople in need of products, and your talent is that product.

If your synopsis intrigues the agent, he will leaf through the script and form a tentative opinion of it. If he likes what he scans, he will diligently read the entire script. And any others you submit.

If his reaction is positive, you will get a call or a letter from him. Otherwise, your portfolio will be returned—in the stamped self-addressed envelope which you provided. If the latter happens, don't despair. There are all those other agents, and no one agent's judgment is infallible, as agents are the first to admit.

You might consider rewriting your screenplay into a play to be presented by your local little-theater group. This is really a great help to a budding dramatist, whether you want to write for the theater, movies, or television. If you live in a community in which a local TV channel will take chances on new plays, you might ask them to produce your play. Let the agent you seek know that it has been produced, and send along all (favorable) reviews.

Finally, we advise you to put yourself on the scene. If it is at all possible, go to Beverly Hills, California, where the action is. Even if you have to hock your Honda, use your vacation time to visit agents, with your scripts in hand, because an exchange of ideas in a personal confrontation will be invaluable to you. Be prepared to sell yourself as a writer, and this includes an ability to stop talking long enough to listen to what the agent suggests or advises. Don't go in with the idea that Norman Lear and Abby Mann are small stuff compared with your monumental genius and that you have no need for advice. For the present, put yourself at the agent's disposal; later he will work for you.

If you cannot stay in the Los Angeles area, your agent will submit scripts sent from wherever you live and he may be able to arrange assignments which you can write there. Supply him with at least six copies of any script(s) which he is optimistic about submitting.

If you are a film buff, you will know the styles of various directors. If you feel that one of them will be more compatible with your work than others, call the Directors Guild of America in Los Angeles (phone: [213] 656–1220) and ask for the name, address, and phone number of his agent. If they have it they will be glad to give it to you. Send the agent your script with a covering letter asking that it be given to the director, and enclose an outline or a synopsis of the screenplay, plus a stamped self-addressed envelope. If the director is interested, a mighty blow has been struck for your career in screenwriting.

The same is true of the Screen Actors Guild in Los Angeles (phone: [213] 876–3030), if you think there is a role in your screenplay which will appeal to a certain actor/actress. Find out who his/her agent is and send your script to him. If he is a reputable agent he will get your script to that client.

If it is a dynamite script you will hear from the agent in a reasonable period of time, one that won't have you crawling the walls. Otherwise, you may have to make periodic inquiries about its status.

Above all, communicate with your agent. We remind you that he is continuously under pressure, but don't hesitate to call him. If he is worth his salt, he will often be out of the office or on the phone (making deals for clients), so do exert some patience along with your persistence.

"SPEC" SCRIPTS

All scripts written on speculation, which your first ones will be, may not sell, but it is quite possible that the writer will be "bought." In this case, you might be asked to rewrite that particular script or, on the strength of its merits, to submit others. Or you may be assigned to work on other scripts. This is particularly true in television.

The producer is not allowed, according to Writers Guild of America rules, to ask you to write a spec script without compensation. However, as a Guild member you may write spec scripts which are not an inducement from a signator producer. But if the script is accepted you may not rewrite at their request without compensation.

Charlotte Brown, co-producer of the *Rhoda* shows, prefers scripts written on speculation because they show her that a writer not only understands the continuing characters in the series but can write good situations and dialog. Perhaps she will not produce the spec script, but if the writing appeals to her she might "buy" the writer instead.

Agents do not always recognize this and fail to offer spec scripts to established shows. Producers and story editors never see them. So your agent may need prodding.

COPYRIGHTS, CONTRACTS, OPTIONS

If you want to copyright your script, write to the United States Copyright Office, Washington, D.C. 20599. Ask for Form D, Application for Registration of a Claim to Copyright in a dramatic or dramatico-musical composition. Enclose a check or money order for $6. Return the signed form with your complete script; a treatment, outline, or synopsis cannot be copyrighted. Many screenwriters do not copyright their scripts, because once the script is sold to a studio or a producer the copyright becomes the property of the purchaser. However, it is likely, so ponderous is the film industry machinery, that two or more years will pass before your script is actually bought, so it is a good idea in the interim to secure your legal ownership. Incidentally, don't write the copyright number on the cover of your script.

An accepted procedure is simply to send the script by registered mail to yourself. Keep it (unopened) with the registration receipt in a safe place until it is needed, if ever.

Under the WRITERS GUILD OF AMERICA, WEST section in this chapter you will find a copy of the manuscript registration service.

Eric Weissmann, an attorney for many film industry clients, explains in the interview at the end of this chapter how you can best protect yourself in contract or option negotiations.

The most common purchase of a newcomer's property is by option, usually taken by the purchaser for eighteen months, never less than a year. This gives him an opportunity to try to put together a deal that will eventually put your screenplay on the screen.

Your agent will handle all details concerning contracts or options for you. Or you may want to secure the services of an attorney who is familiar with the economic intricacies of moviemaking.

Another way to protect the ownership of your script is by registering it with the Writers Guild of America. Details are given below.

WRITERS GUILD OF AMERICA, WEST

There is a vast amount of material published by the Writers Guild which is extremely helpful to writers. Because of space limitations, it is impossible to reproduce it here, but we have selected the material which is most important to beginning screenwriters. The offices of Writers Guild of America, West, Inc., are located in Los Angeles (phone: [213] 550–1000). All mail should be sent to 8955 Beverly Boulevard, Los Angeles, California. It is affiliated with Writers Guild of America, East: 22 W. 48th Street, New York, New York 10036 (phone: [212] 575–5060). The New York address should be used by anyone living east of the Mississippi River.

A person is eligible for membership in the Guild by reason of obtaining employment as a writer or selling unpublished and unproduced literary material in the motion picture, television, or radio industry. The employer or the purchaser need not be a signatory in order for such a person to qualify for membership in the Guild, but no member of the Guild may render writing services for, or sell literary material to, a non-signatory.

From the membership department of the Guild you will receive the following form (with enclosures) upon request.

MEMBERSHIP FORM

The Guild represents writers primarily for the purpose of collective bargaining in the motion picture, television, and radio industries.

☐ We do not obtain employment for writers, nor offer writing instruction or advice nor do we accept or handle material for submission to production companies. Literary material should be submitted directly to the production companies or through a literary agent.

☐ Enclosed is a current list of literary agencies.

☐ Our Television Market List may be obtained by sending one dollar and addressing your request to the attention of Blanche Baker.

☐ Information on our Registration Service is enclosed.

☐ The minimum requirement for membership in the Guild is that you have had employment as a writer for screen, television, or radio or that you have sold original material to one of these media. The initiation fee is $400.00. Your application must be supported with a copy of your contract or other acceptable evidence of such employment or sale.

☐ For information on writing courses, we suggest you communicate with your State college or university or with your local Board of Education.

☐ Guild policy precludes us from giving out names, addresses, or phone numbers of any of our members. Correspondence* may be addressed to a member in care of the Guild and will be forwarded promptly.

MANUSCRIPT REGISTRATION SERVICE

PURPOSE   The Guild's Registration Service has been set up to assist members and non-members in establishing the completion date and the identity of their literary property.

VALUE   Registration does not confer any statutory protection. It merely provides evidence of the writer's prior claim to authorship of the literary material involved and of the date of its completion. An author has certain rights under the law the moment his work is completed. It is therefore important that the date of completion be legally established. The Registration Office does not make comparisons of registration deposits to determine similarity between works, nor does it give legal opinions or advice.

COVERAGE   Since the value of registration is merely to supply evidence, it cannot protect what the law does not protect. Registration with the Guild does not protect titles (neither does registration with the United States Copyright Office).

PROCEDURE FOR DEPOSIT   Effective February 1, 1976, the following restrictions will be placed on material accepted for registration: One (1) copy, 8½ × 11 inch paper only, unbound. Use of one side only, no onion skin paper and preferably white for best micro-film results. When it is received, the property is dated, given a registration number and put on file. A receipt is returned. Notice of registration shall consist of the wording REGISTERED WGAw NO._____ and be applied upon the title page or the page immediately following. Formats, outlines, synopses or general descriptions of theatrical motion pictures, radio and television programs are registrable. Each property must be registered separately. (Exception: two episodes of an existing series may

*First-class postage.

be deposited as a single registration.) Be sure that the name under which you register is your full legal name. The use of pseudonyms, pen names or initials may require proof of identity if you want to recover the material left on deposit.

DURATION   The Guild reserves the right to micro-film the manuscript and to destroy the manuscript at any time thereafter. You hereby authorize the Guild to destroy the manuscript or the micro-film without notice to you on the expiration of ten years from the date hereof. You may however renew the registration for an additional ten years if before the expiration of the first ten year period you pay the then applicable renewal fee and get a written receipt therefor. Fee should accompany request for renewal.

LOCATION OF REGISTRATION OFFICE:
9038 MELROSE AVENUE (at Doheny)
LOS ANGELES, CA 90069

HOURS: 10 A.M. - 12 NOON
2 P.M. - 5 P.M.   MONDAY THRU FRIDAY

ALL MAIL SHOULD BE SENT TO THE BEVERLY BOULEVARD ADDRESS

PROCEDURE FOR WITHDRAWAL   The registered copy left on deposit cannot be returned to the author without defeating the purpose of registration, the point being that evidence should be available, if necessary, that the material has been in the Guild's charge since the date of deposit.

However, if the author finds it necessary to have the copy returned to him, at least twenty-four (24) hours notice of intended withdrawal must be given to the Guild. If the manuscript is on micro-film, a per page charge at then current rates will be made at time of withdrawal. A manuscript will be surrendered only to the author upon presentation of the original receipt and proper identification, or, to another bearing a written authorization signed by the author. Where there are co-authors, written consent of all parties must be provided. And where the author is deceased, proof of death and consent of heirs must be obtained. In no event, except under these provisions, shall any of the material be allowed to be taken from the Guild office unless a court order has been acquired.

If any person other than the author named in the registration shall request to see either the material deposited, the registration receipt, the registration envelope or any other material, such request shall be denied unless a court order is presented in connection therewith.

FEES $4.00 for members of WGA and WGGB

$10.00 for non-members
$1.00 for members when registration is renewed*
$4.00 for members when registration is renewed**
$1.50 for non-members when registration is renewed*
$10.00 for non-members when registration is renewed**
<u>FEE MUST ACCOMPANY REQUEST FOR REGISTRATION</u>

GUILD FUNCTIONS AND SERVICES

1. <u>CONTRACTS</u>
   a. Negotiation of Basic Agreements in screen, television (both live and film), radio and staff agreements (news and continuity writers).
   b. Administration of same:
      (1) Handling of writer claims.
      (2) Checking of individual writer contracts for violations of the MBA.
      (3) Enforcement of Working Rules.
      (4) Processing of Grievances.
      (5) Distribution of Unfair Lists and Strike Lists.
      (6) Arbitrations under the MBA.
      (7) Collection and processing of television and motion picture residuals.
      (8) Pension Plan.
      (9) Health and Welfare Plan.
      (10) Signatory lists.
2. <u>CREDITS</u>
   a. Receipt of tentative notices.
   b. Arbitration of protests.
   c. Maintenance of Credit records.
   d. Distribution of Credits Manual.
   e. Credit information to members and to producers and agents.
3. <u>ORIGINAL MATERIAL</u>
   a. Registration.
   b. Collaboration Agreements.
   c. Settlement of disputes (Committee on Original Material).
   d. Copyright information and legislation.
4. <u>AGENTS</u>
   a. Negotiation of Basic Agreement with Agents.
   b. Recording, filing, and administration of individual agreements between writers and agents.
   c. Distribution of lists of authorized agents.
   d. Arbitration function in disputes between writers and agents.
5. <u>EMPLOYMENT</u>
   a. Compilation and distribution of TV Market Lists to members.

*Registered prior to February 1, 1968
**Registered after February 1, 1968

   b. Compilation and circulation of motion picture and TV credits lists to producers and agents.
   c. Compilation and circulation of statistical data re members where requested.
6. <u>INFORMATION</u>
   a. Inquiries by producers re member credits and contract provisions and agents.
   b. Inquiries by members and non-members re production data and contract provisions.
7. <u>AFFILIATION AND COOPERATION</u>
   a. British Writers Guild
   b. Australian Writers Guild
   c. Canadian Writers Guild
   d. Motion Picture and Television Relief Fund
   e. Permanent Charities Committee
   f. American Film Institute
   g. Open Door Program
   h. Other industry functions and services
8. <u>PUBLIC RELATIONS</u>
   a. Publications—Newsletter
   b. Trade press
   c. TV forums
   d. Annual Awards Event
9. <u>CREDIT UNION</u>
   a. Loans
   b. Investments
   c. Life Insurance
10. <u>GROUP INSURANCE</u>
   a. Life Insurance
   a. Disability; Hospitalization; Major Medical
11. <u>LEGISLATION</u>
   a. Copyright
   b. Censorship
   c. Taxation
   d. Unemployment Compensation
12. <u>FILM SOCIETY</u>
13. <u>WORKSHOP PROGRAMS</u>
14. <u>SUPPORT OF FREEDOM OF EXPRESSION</u>
   a. Litigation
   b. Press
   c. Other
15. <u>DIRECTORY</u>
16. <u>COMMITTEES</u>
   a. Writer Conferences
   b. Social Activities
17. <u>WRITERS GUILD THEATRE</u>

a. Screenings
b. Rental
c. Meeting Rooms

MEMBERSHIP—ARTICLE IV

ARTICLE IV

Membership

Section 1. General

There shall be four classes of membership in this Guild, which classes shall be denominated Associate, Current, Non-Current, and Withdrawn. Upon application to and acceptance in the Guild the applicant shall be designated either an Associate member or a Current member in accordance with the provisions of Sections 2 and 3 of this Article. In the event a member shall fail to maintain his Current membership in the Guild as provided in Section 4 of this Article, he shall nevertheless continue as a Non-Current member.

Section 2. Eligibility for Associate Membership

Any person engaged to write literary or dramatic material for, and any author of unpublished and unproduced literary or dramatic material as to which rights are sold or licensed or granted for use in the motion picture, radio, television industries or other related industries, as such industries are presently constituted or as they may hereafter be constituted or reconstituted, shall be eligible for Associate membership in this Guild.

Section 3. Eligibility for Current Status

The Unit Credit System hereafter set forth is designed to measure as accurately and fairly as possible the nature and kind of writing done. It shall be the duty of the Board of Directors to review the system and the designated units of credit from time to time. And when, in the judgment of the Board of Directors, changes occur in the industry or otherwise which warrant consideration by the membership, the Board of Directors shall place before the membership appropriate recommendations.

Any person shall attain Current status in the Guild if during the preceding two years he has accumulated an aggregate of twelve (12) Units of Credit as hereafter set forth, which units are based upon work completed under contract of employment or upon the sale or licensing of previously unpublished and unproduced literary or dramatic material provided, however, said employment, sale or licensing is within the jurisdiction of the Guild as provided in its collective bargaining contracts.

(a) If a person is employed within the Guild's jurisdiction on a week-to-week or term basis he shall be entitled to one Unit of Credit for each complete week of such employment.

(b) Units of Credit may also be attained in accordance with the following schedule:

One Unit

Episode in series for which writer receives "Created By" credit.
Comedy-Variety Program: one unit per week of employment or one unit per show, whichever is more.

Two Units

Story for theatrical motion picture short subject.
Story for TV or radio program one-half hour or less.

Three Units

Screenplay for theatrical motion picture short subject.
Teleplay or radio play for program one-half hour or less.
Television format or presentation for a new series.

Four Units

Story for one-hour TV or radio program.

Five Units

Story and teleplay or story and radio play one-half hour or less.

Six Units

Story for 90-minute teleplay or radio play.
One-hour teleplay or radio play.
Comedy-variety special regardless of length.

Eight Units

Story for theatrical motion picture.
Story for two-hour TV or radio program.

Nine Units

90-minute teleplay or radio play.

Ten Units

One-hour story and teleplay or story and radio play.

Full Qualification For Current Status

Screenplay for theatrical motion picture.
Two-hour teleplay or two-hour radio play.
90-minute story and teleplay or story and radio play.

(c) A rewrite is entitled to one-half the number of units allotted to its particular category in subdivision (b) above.

(d) A polish is entitled to one-quarter the number of units allotted to its particular category in subdivision (b) above.

(e) Sale of an option earns one-half the number of units allotted to its particular category in subdivision (b) above, subject to a maximum entitlement of four (4) such units in any one year.

(f) If a person under an employment contract writes material or sells or licenses previously unpublished or unproduced material intended as a pilot episode for a television series, he shall receive twice the number of units of credit applicable to similar material for a television program of equal length.

(g) Where writers collaborate on the same project each shall be accorded the appropriate number of units designated in subdivisions (b) through (f) above.

(h) All work done by a writer prior to acceptance into the Guild, in the case only of flat deal employment or sale of material, qualifies for one-half the applicable number of units in subdivisions (b) through (g) above for the purposes of achieving Current status. However in exceptional cases the Board of Directors, acting upon a recommendation of the Membership and Finance Committee, shall have power to grant the full number of units applicable in subdivisions (b) through (g).

(i) Unit credit for the writing or sale or licensing of material for pay television shall be determined by the Board of Directors. In addition, the Board of Directors shall have the authority, in any case not covered by this Section 3, to make specific Unit Credit determinations applicable to any such work. Unit Credit determinations made by the Board of Directors shall be submitted for approval by the membership at the first annual or special membership meeting following such determinations.

(j) For the sole purpose of determining Unit Credits where applicable the "Full Qualification" designation for screenplay for theatrical motion picture, two-hour teleplay or radio play and 90-minute story and teleplay or story and radio play, shall be deemed to be the equivalent of twelve (12) Units of Credit.

Section 4.   Duration of Current Status

(a) Any Current member shall become a Non-Current member if, during any three consecutive years, he does not earn at least six (6) Units of Credit. A Non-Current member shall be reinstated to Current status if during any three (3) consecutive years as a Non-Current member, he earns six (6) Units of Credit. As of the date of adoption of this Constitution and thereafter, Current membership shall be extended one additional year for each six years of Current (or Active) membership in Writers Guild of America, west, Inc. or Writers Guild of America, east, Inc., provided, however, that such extensions will not be granted for a total of more than three years and will only apply to a member who is Current at the time they are granted. Additional years of extended Current membership shall not count in any calculation for a further extension.

(b) Any member with Current status who does not continue his Current status by reason of the foregoing provisions of this Section 4 shall maintain his Current status in the Guild for the sole purpose of participating in any voluntary member-paid insurance benefits which the Guild may presently or hereafter obtain.

Section 5.   Non-Resident Writers

The Board of Directors shall have the power to admit to Current status in the Guild any person who is employed in the United States in the motion picture, radio or television industries or related industries as a writer and who is an Active or Current member in good standing of any organization of writers which includes among its purposes and powers the representation of the professional and economic interests of writers employed outside the United States and which does not purport to represent writers employed in the United States and which has adopted previous provisions substantially identical to this Section with regard to members of this Guild. The Current status of any such person shall be limited to the duration of his initial employment as a writer in the Guild's jurisdiction plus an additional period to be granted at the discretion of the Board of Directors not to exceed six months or the balance of his stay in the United States, whichever shall be the shorter period of time.

Upon commencement of work in this Guild's jurisdiction such non-resident writers shall apply for and may be admitted to membership in this Guild without the obligation to pay the initiation fee specified in Article VIII Section 5 of this Constitution although all other financial obligations specified in said Article VIII shall pertain to said writers.

Section 6.   Duration of Associate and Non-Current Status;
Eligibility for Withdrawn Membership

(a) Associate—an Associate member who has never become Current in the Guild shall be dropped from membership if he shall not be employed as a writer in any field over which the Guild exercises jurisdiction or if no unpublished and unproduced literary or dramatic material to which he has contributed has been sold or rights therein licensed during any period of three consecutive years. The Board of Directors may, for good cause shown, extend such membership for any period it may deem proper, providing such extension is approved by a two-thirds' vote of the Board of Directors.

GUILD SHOP INFORMATION

a. If a writer is not a member of the Guild at the time of his employment and although required by the provisions of his employment agreement to do so, fails or refuses to become a member of the Guild in good standing within the 30 days abovementioned, provided that within 15 days after written notice thereof from the Guild to the Company, the Company shall either terminate such employment or shall pay or cause to be paid the initiation fees and dues of the writer in the manner, within the time, and subject to the provisions of subsection 5.b. hereof relating to the payment of dues. If the Company elects to and does pay such initiation fees and dues, such writer shall be deemed to be a member of the Guild in good standing, but only for the period necessary to permit him to complete the performance of his services in connection with the then current assignment. The Company may use this exception only once for any particular person.

b. To a writer whom the Company is required to employ as a condition of the sale or license of material, provided that within 15 days after written notice from the Guild to the Company that such writer is not a member of the Guild in good standing, the Company shall either terminate such employment, or shall pay or cause to be paid the initiation fees and dues that the writer would otherwise be required to pay hereunder during such employment, in the manner, within the time, and subject to the provisions of subsection 5.b. hereof relating to the payment of dues. However, the writers employed by the Company within the exception provided for in this subparagraph (b) shall not exceed 10% of the total number of writers in the employ of the Company. For the purpose of such computation if the Company has in its employ at any time less than 10 writers, then 1 of such writers so employed may fall within this exception. Promptly following the employment of any writer claimed by the Company to be within this exception, the Company will notify the Guild in writing of the name of the writer employed, the date of the employment agreement and the fact that the Company claims that such writer is an exception hereunder. For the purpose of such computation a writer who is employed under an exclusive contract by a Company shall be regarded as being employed by the Company at all times during the term of such contract, including periods during which the writer may be on layoff and periods during which such contract may be suspended by reason of illness or default of the writer or otherwise. The writer shall be regarded as continuing in the employ of the Company by which he is employed regardless of the fact that his services may be loaned to another Company.

5. If during any time that a writer is employed by the Company under a contract of employment such writer is or becomes a member of the Guild in good standing and if such writer shall subsequently and before his employment under such contract terminates, cease to be a member of the Guild in good standing then:

a. If such writer has ceased or shall cease to be a member for any reason other than his failure to pay dues, such writer shall, for the purposes of this Basic Agreement, be deemed to remain a member of the Guild in good standing throughout the writer's employment under said contract of employment as the same may be extended or renewed pursuant to any provisions or options therein contained.

b. If he has ceased or shall cease to be a member in good standing by reason of his failure to pay dues, and if the Guild gives the Company written notice of that fact within three business days after such writer is first named on the weekly list provided for in Article 3 A.1. of this Basic Agreement.

FILM MINIMUMS

WRITER'S FLAT DEAL CONTRACT

(Short Form; complete screenplay, no options)

EMPLOYMENT AGREEMENT between _____
(hereinafter sometimes referred to as "Company" and _____
(hereinafter sometimes referred to as "Writer"), dated this _____
day of_____, 19____.

1. The Company employs the Writer to write a complete and finished screen-

WGA 1977 THEATRICAL AND TELEVISION BASIC AGREEMENT
THEATRICAL COMPENSATION

EMPLOYMENT, FLAT DEALS	Effective 3/2/77 - 3/1/79		Effective 3/2/79 - 3/1/80		Effective 3/2/80 - 3/1/81	
	LOW	HIGH	LOW	HIGH	LOW	HIGH
A. Screenplay, Including Treatment	$11,211	$20,821	$12,220	$22,695	$14,175	$26,326
Installments:						
Delivery of Treatment	4,204	6,406	4,582	6,983	5,315	8,100
Delivery of First Draft Screenplay	5,046	9,610	5,500	10,475	6,380	12,151
Delivery of Final Draft Screenplay	1,961	4,805	2,138	5,237	2,480	6,075
B. Screenplay, Excluding Treatment	$ 7,008	$14,414	$ 7,639	$15,711	$ 8,861	$18,225
Installments:						
Delivery of First Draft Screenplay	5,046	9,610	5,500	10,475	6,380	12,151
Delivery of Final Draft Screenplay	1,962	4,804	2,139	5,236	2,481	6,074
C. Additional Compensation for Story Included in Screenplay	$ 1,602	$ 3,203	$ 1,746	$ 3,491	$ 2,025	$ 4,050
D. Story or Treatment	$ 4,204	$ 6,406	$ 4,582	$ 6,983	$ 5,315	$ 8,100
E. Original Treatment	$ 5,806	$ 9,610	$ 6,329	$10,475	$ 7,342	$12,151
F. First Draft Screenplay, With or Without Option For Final Draft Screenplay						
First Draft Screenplay	$ 5,046	$ 9,610	$ 5,500	$10,475	$ 6,380	$12,151
Final Draft Screenplay	$ 3,363	$ 6,406	$ 3,666	$ 6,983	$ 4,253	$ 8,100
G. Rewrite of Screenplay	$ 4,204	$ 6,406	$ 4,582	$ 6,983	$ 5,315	$ 8,100
H. Polish of Screenplay	$ 2,102	$ 3,203	$ 2,291	$ 3,491	$ 2,658	$ 4,050

* LOW BUDGET - Photoplay costing less than $1,000,000

HIGH BUDGET - Photoplay costing $1,000,000 or more

* For special minimum terms applicable to Low Budget Photoplays, see next page.

WGA 1977 THEATRICAL AND TELEVISION BASIC AGREEMENT
THEATRICAL COMPENSATION

SPECIAL MINIMUM TERMS APPLICABLE TO LOW BUDGET PHOTOPLAYS (under $1,000,000)

For details as to applicability of the special Low Budget schedule, contact the Guild.

EMPLOYMENT, FLAT DEALS

	Minimum Compensation	Effective 3/2/77 -3/1/78 Additional Sum Payable on Start of Principal Photography	Effective 3/2/78 - 3/1/79	Effective 3/2/79 - 3/1/80	Effectiv 3/2/80 - 3/1/81
A. Screenplay, Including Treatment	$10,611	$720	$11,407	$12,377	$14,172
Installments:					
Delivery of Treatment	3,979		4,277	4,641	5,314
Delivery of First Draft Screenplay	4,775		5,133	5,569	6,377
Delivery of Final Draft Screenplay	1,857		1,997	2,167	2,481
B. Screenplay, Excluding Treatment	$ 6,632	$451	$ 7,129	$ 7,735	$ 8,857
Installments:					
Delivery of First Draft Screenplay	4,775		5,133	5,569	6,377
Delivery of Final Draft Screenplay	1,857		1,996	2,166	2,480
C. Additional Compensation for Story Included in Screenplay	$ 1,516	$103	$ 1,630	$ 1,769	$ 2,026
D. Story or Treatment	$ 3,979	$271	$ 4,277	$ 4,641	$ 5,314
E. Original Treatment	$ 5,495	$373	$ 5,907	$ 6,409	$ 7,338
F. First Draft Screenplay; With or Without Option for Final Draft Screenplay					
First Draft Screenplay	$ 4,775	$325	$ 5,133	$ 5,569	$ 6,377
Final Draft Screenplay	$ 3,183	$216	$ 3,422	$ 3,713	$ 4,251
G. Rewrite of Screenplay	$ 3,979	$271	$ 4,277	$ 4,641	$ 5,314
H. Polish of Screenplay	$ 1,990	$135	$ 2,139	$ 2,321	$ 2,658

play, presently entitled or designated _____
including the following:

    Treatment
    Original Treatment
    Story
    First draft screenplay   (Draw a line through
    Final draft screenplay   portions not applicable)
    Rewrite of screenplay

2. (a) The Writer represents that (s)he is a member in good standing of the Writers Guild of America, west, Inc. and warrants that he will maintain his membership in Writers Guild of America, west, Inc. in good standing during the term of this employment.

(b) The Company warrants that it is a party to the Writers Guild of America Theatrical and Television Film Basic Agreement of 1973 (which agreement is herein designated "MBA").

(c) Should any of the terms hereof be less advantageous to the Writer than the minimums provided in said MBA, then the terms of the MBA shall supersede such terms hereof.

Without limiting the generality of the foregoing, it is agreed that screen credits for authorship shall be determined pursuant to the provisions of Schedule A of the MBA in accordance with its terms at the time of determination.

3. The Company will pay to the Writer as full compensation for his services hereunder the sum of_____DOLLARS($_____), payable as follows:

(a) Not less than *SEVEN HUNDRED EIGHTY-FIVE DOLLARS ($785.00)* shall be paid not later than the first regular weekly pay day of the Company following the expiration of the first week of the Writer's employment;

(b)_____DOLLARS ($_____) shall be paid within forty-eight (48) hours after delivery of the TREATMENT, ORIGINAL TREATMENT, or STORY, whichever is appropriate, to the Company;

(c)_____DOLLARS ($_____) shall be paid within forty-eight (48) hours after delivery of the FIRST DRAFT SCREENPLAY to the Company; and

(d)_____DOLLARS ($_____) shall be paid within forty-eight (48) hours after delivery of the FINAL DRAFT SCREENPLAY.

(e)_____DOLLARS ($_____) shall be paid within forty-eight (48) hours after delivery of the REWRITE.

4. The Writer will immediately on the execution hereof diligently proceed to render services hereunder and will so continue until such services are completed.

5. On delivery of a treatment to the Company, the Company may call for changes within three (3) days thereafter; if the Company fails in writing to call for any such changes, the treatment shall be deemed approved, and the Writer shall proceed with the first draft screenplay based on such treatment or adaptation.

On delivery of a first draft screenplay to the Company, the Company may call for changes within three (3) days thereafter; if the Company fails in writing to call for any such changes, the first draft screenplay shall be deemed approved, and the Writer shall proceed with the final draft screenplay.

On delivery of the final draft screenplay to the Company, the Company may call for changes within three (3) days thereafter; if the Company fails in writing to call for any such changes, the final draft screenplay shall be deemed approved.

6. This contract is entire, that is, the services contemplated hereunder include all of the writing necessary to complete the final screenplay above described, and this Agreement contemplates payment of the entire agreed compensation.

_____   _____
(Company)   (Writer)

By _____   Address _____
Title _____   _____
Address _____   _____

_____

WRITERS' REPRESENTATIVES

Unless otherwise stated, all addresses are in Los Angeles, California.

ABRAMS-RUBALOFF & ASSOCIATES
                    273-5711
9012 Beverly Blvd. (90048)
ADAMS, BRET, LIMITED . .   656-6420
8282 Sunset Blvd. (90046)
36 E. 61st St.,   (212) 752-7864
New York, New York (10021)
ADAMS, RAY & ROSENBERG 278-3000
9200 Sunset Blvd., PH 25 (90069)
AIMÉE ENTERTAINMENT
ASSOCIATION   872-0374
14241 Ventura Blvd.,   990-6996
Sherman Oaks, Calif. (91423)
ALVARADO, CARLOS, AGENCY
                    652-0272
8820 Sunset Blvd. (90069)
AMBER, VELVET, AGENCY   464-8184
6515 Sunset Blvd., Suite 200A
(90028)

AMSEL, FRED & ASSOCIATES 277-2035
312 S. Beverly Dr., Suite R,
Beverly Hills, Calif. (90212)
ARCARA, BAUMAN & HILLER ARTISTS'
MANAGERS   271-5601
9220 Sunset Blvd. (90069)
850 7th Ave., Suite 1201
New York, New York (10019)
                    (212) 757-0098
ARTISTS CAREER MANAGEMENT
                    278-9157
9157 Sunset Blvd., #206 (90069)
ASSOCIATED BOOKING CORPORATION
                    273-5600
9595 Wilshire Blvd., Beverly Hills,
Calif. (90212)
BARR, RICKEY/GILLY, GEORGIA
                    659-0141

8721 Sunset Blvd., Suite 210
(90069)
BARSKIN AGENCY, THE . .   657-5740
8730 Sunset Blvd., Suite #501
(90069)
BART/LEVY ASSOCIATES, INC.
550-1060
9169 Sunset Blvd. (90069)
BEAKEL & JENNINGS AGENCY
ARTISTS' MANAGERS . . .   274-5418
9615 Brighton Way, Suite 314,
Beverly Hills, Calif. (90210)
BELCOURT ARTISTS   276-6205
222 N. Canon Dr., Suite 204
Beverly Hills, Calif. (90210)
BELLEVUE LITERARY AGENCY
478-9470
Kirkeby Center, Suite 1034
10889 Wilshire Blvd. (90024)
BLAKE, WILLIAM, AGENCY/WEST
TALENT INTERNATIONAL   274-0321
1888 Century Park East (90067)
BLOOM, BECKETT, LEVY & SHORR
553-4850
449 S. Beverly Dr., Beverly Hills,
Calif. (90212)
BLUMENTHAL ARTISTS AGENCY
656-1451
435 S. La Cienega Blvd. (90048)
BRADY, CHRISTINA, AGENCY 473-2708
11818 Wilshire Blvd. (90025)
BRAND AGENCY   657-2870
8721 Sunset Blvd. (90069)
BRANDON & BARAD ASSOCIATES
273-6173
9046 Sunset Blvd. (90069)
BRESLER, WOLFF, COTA &
LIVINGSTON.   278-3200
190 N. Canon Dr., Beverly Hills,
Calif. (90210)
BREWIS, ALEX, AGENCY. .   274-9874
8721 Sunset Blvd. (90069)
BRIDGETOWN MUSIC CORPORATION
333-5288
723½ N. Glendora Ave.,   283-1830
La Puente, Calif. (91744)

BROWN, NED, INCORPORATED
276-1131
407 N. Maple Dr., Suite 228,
Beverly Hills, Calif. (90210)
CALDER AGENCY, THE . .   652-3380
8749 Sunset Blvd. (90069)
CAMBRIDGE COMPANY, THE 657-2125
9000 Sunset Blvd.,   666-1920
Suite 814 (90069)
CARTER AGENCY, INC., THE 277-2683
1801 Avenue of the Stars, Suite 640
(90067)
CENTURY ARTISTS, LTD. .   273-4366
9744 Wilshire Blvd., Suite 206
Beverly Hills, Calif. (90212)
CHANDLER, RITA, AGENCY 656-4042
8282 Sunset Blvd. (90046)
CHARTER MANAGEMENT .   278-1690
9000 Sunset Blvd. (90069)
CHARTWELL ARTISTS, LTD. 553-3600
1901 Avenue of the Stars (90067)
CHASIN-PARK-CITRON AGENCY
273-7190
9255 Sunset Blvd. (90069)
COLLIER, SHIRLEY, AGENCY 270-4500
1127 Stradella Rd. (90024)
(Representatives in all foreign
countries)
COLTON, KINGSLEY & ASSOCIATES,
INC.   277-5491
321 S. Beverly Dr., Beverly Hills,
Calif. (90212)
COMPASS MANAGEMENT, INC.
271-5122
211 S. Beverly Dr.
Beverly Hills, Calif. (90212)
CONNOR-CORFINO, ASSOCIATES, INC.
981-1133
14241 Ventura Blvd. Sherman
Oaks, Calif. (91423)
CONTEMPORARY-KORMAN ARTISTS,
LTD.   278-8250
Contemporary Artists Building
132 Lasky Dr., Beverly Hills, Calif.
(90212)

CONWAY, BEN & ASSOC.. .   271-8133
  999 N. Doheny Dr., # 403 (90069)
COOPER, DOUG, AGENCY .   980-6100
  10850 Riverside Dr., Suite 601-A
  N. Hollywood, Calif. (91602)
CORALIE JR. AGENCY . . .   766-9501
  4789 Vineland,   681-8281
  N. Hollywood, Calif. (91602)
COSAY, WERNER & ASSOCIATES
                               550-1535
  9744 Wilshire Blvd., Beverly Hills,
  Calif. (90212)
CREATIVE ARTISTS AGENCY, INC.
                               277-4545
  1888 Century Park East, Suite 1400
  (90067)
CUMBER, LIL, ATTRACTIONS AGENCY
                               469-1919
  6515 Sunset Blvd., Suite 408
  (90028)
DADE/ROSEN ASSOCIATES   278-7077
  999 N. Doheny Dr., Suite 102
  (90069)
DANSON ARTISTS' AGENCY   769-3100
  10732 Riverside Dr.,
  N. Hollywood, Calif. (91602)
DIAMOND ARTISTS, LTD.   654-5960
  8400 Sunset Blvd. (90069)
  119 W. 57th St.,   (212) CI7-3025
  New York, New York (10019)
EISENBACK-GREENE-DUCHOW, INC.
                               659-3420
  760 N. La Cienega Blvd. (90069)
FCA AGENCY, INC.   278-1460
  9000 Sunset Blvd. (90069)
FERRELL, CAROL, AGENCY   466-8311
  6331 Hollywood Blvd., #828
  (90028)
FIELDS, JACK & ASSOCIATES 278-1333
  9255 Sunset Blvd., Suite 1105
  (90069)
FILM ARTISTS MANAGEMENT
  ENTERPRISES, INC.   656-7590
  8278 Sunset Blvd. (90046)
FISCHER, SY, COMPANY, THE 273-3575
  9255 Sunset Blvd. (90069)

FLEMING, PETER, AGENCY   271-5693
  9046 Sunset Blvd., Suite 206
  (90069)
GARRICK, DALE, INTERNATIONAL
  AGENCY   657-2661
  8831 Sunset Blvd. (90069)
GERSH, PHIL, AGENCY, INC. 274-6611
  222 N. Canon Dr., Beverly Hills,
  Calif. (90210)
GIBSON, CARTER J., AGENCY 274-8813
  9000 Sunset Blvd. (90069)
GOLDFARB/LEWIS AGENCY   659-5955
  Falcon Gold, Inc.
  8733 Sunset Blvd. (90069)
GOLDSTEIN, ALLEN & ASSOC., LTD.
                               278-5005
  9301 Wilshire Blvd., Beverly Hills,
  Calif. (90210)
GORDEAN-FRIEDMAN AGENCY, INC.,
  THE   273-4195
  9229 Sunset Blvd. (90069)
GRANITE AGENCY, THE . .   934-8383
  1920 S. La Cienega Blvd., Suite 205
  (90034)
GRASHIN, MAURI, AGENCY   652-5168
  8730 Sunset Blvd. (90069)
GREEN, IVAN, AGENCY, THE 277-1541
  1900 Avenue of the Stars, Suite
  1070 (90067)
GREENE, GLORIA, CREATIVE
  EXPRESSIONS   274-7661
  439 La Cienega Blvd. (90048)
GROSSMAN, LARRY & ASSOCIATES,
  INC.   550-8127
  9229 Sunset Blvd., Suite 502
  (90069)
GROSSMAN-STALMASTER AGENCY
                               657-3040
  8730 Sunset Blvd., Suite 405
  (90069)
HALLIBURTON, JEANNE, AGENCY
                               466-6138
  5205 Hollywood Blvd., Suite 203
  (90027)
HALSEY, REECE, AGENCY   652-2409
  8733 Sunset Blvd. (90069) 652-7595

HAMILBURG, MITCHELL J., AGENCY
657-1501
292 S. La Cienega Blvd., Suite 212,
Beverly Hills, Calif. (90211)

HENDERSON/HOGAN AGENCY, INC.
274-7815
247 S. Beverly Dr., Beverly Hills,
Calif. (90212)
200 W. 57th St.   (212) 765-5190
New York, New York (10019)

HOLLYWOOD, DANIEL, THEATRICAL
MANAGEMENT, LTD. . . .   550-0570
9200 Sunset Blvd., Suite 808
(90069)

HUSSONG, ROBERT G., AGENCY, INC.
655-2534
8271 Melrose Ave., Suite 108
(90046)

HYLAND-DE LAUER, LITERARY
AGENCY   278-0300
8961 Sunset Blvd. (90069)

I.M. AGENCY LTD.   277-1376
1888 Century Park East (90067)

INTERNATIONAL CREATIVE
MANAGEMENT   550-4000
8899 Beverly Blvd. (90048)
40 West 57th Street,
New York, New York (10019)
(212) 556-5600

INTERNATIONAL LITERARY AGENTS,
LTD.   274-8779
Peri Winkler
9601 Wilshire Blvd., Suite 300,
Beverly Hills, Calif. (90210)

IRWIN, LOU, AGENCY . . .   553-4775
9901 Durant Dr., Suite A,
Beverly Hills, Calif. (90212)

ISER, BEVERLY KAHN, AGENCY
657-8693
9701 Wilshire Blvd., Suite 710
Beverly Hills, Calif. (90212)

JACKSON, IONE J.   293-8833
4306 S. Crenshaw Blvd. (90008)

JOSEPH, L.H., JR. & ASSOCIATES
651-2322
8344 Melrose Ave. (90069)

KAHN-PENNEY AGENCY . .   656-4042
8282 Sunset Blvd. (90046)

KANE, MERRILY, AGENCY   550-8874
9171 Wilshire Blvd., Suite 310,
Beverly Hills, Calif. (90210)

KARLIN, LARRY, AGENCY   550-0570
9200 Sunset Blvd. (90069)

KOHNER, PAUL-LEVY, MICHAEL
AGENCY   550-1060
9169 Sunset Blvd. (90069)

KURLAND, NORMAN, AGENCY, THE
274-8921
9701 Wilshire Blvd., Suite 800
Beverly Hills, Calif. (90212)

LARSEN, MICHAEL-POMADA,
ELIZABETH, LITERARY AGENTS
(415) 673-0939
1029 Jones St., San Francisco,
Calif. (94109)

LAZAR, IRVING PAUL, AGENCY
275-6153
211 S. Beverly Dr., Beverly Hills,
Calif. (90212)

LENNY, JACK, ASSOCIATES   271-2174
9701 Wilshire Blvd., Beverly Hills,
Calif. (90212)
140 W. 58th Street,
New York, New York (10019)
(212) 582-0270

LEVEE, GORDON B., AGENCY 652-0012
8721 Sunset Blvd., Suite 103
(90069)

LEVERING, LILLIA ARTISTS'
MANAGER   874-9591
P.O. Box 1447 (90028)

LEWIS, HENRY, AGENCY   275-5129
9172 Sunset Blvd. (90069)

LITTMAN, ROBERT, COMPANY, THE
278-1572
409 N. Camden Drive, Beverly
Hills, Calif. (90210)

LOO, BESSIE, AGENCY . . .   657-5888
8746 Sunset Blvd. (90069)

LOVELL & ASSOCIATES . .   659-8476
8730 Sunset Blvd. (90069)

LYONS, GRACE, AGENCY   652-5290
  8732 Sunset Blvd. (90069)
MAJOR TALENT AGENCY, INC.
                          820-5841
  12301 Wilshire Blvd., Suite 515
  (90025)
MARKSON, RAYA L. LITERARY
  AGENCY   552-2083
  Artists' Manager   997-6699
                            788-6788
  1888 Century Park East, Suite 1015
  (90067)
McCLENDON, ERNESTINE,
  ENTERPRISES, INC.   654-4425
  8440 Sunset Blvd., Suite M-5
  (90069)
McHUGH, JAMES, AGENCY   651-2770
  8150 Beverly Blvd., Suite 206
  (90048)
McKIERNAN & GURROLA   746-3550
  1150 S. Olive St., Suite 1400
  (90015)
MEDFORD, BEN, AGENCY   271-7021
  9440 Santa Monica Blvd., Suite 403
  (92120)
MEIKLEJOHN, WILLIAM, ASSOCIATES
                          273-2566
  9250 Wilshire Blvd., Beverly Hills,
  Calif. (90212)
MESSENGER, FRED, AGENCY   654-3800
  8265 Sunset Blvd. (90046)
M.E.W. COMPANY 653-4731
  151 N. San Vicente Blvd., Beverly
  Hills, Calif. (90211)
MILLER, STUART M., CO., THE
                          659-8131
  8693 Wilshire Blvd., Suite 206
  Beverly Hills, Calif. (90211)
MISHKIN AGENCY, INC., THE 274-5261
  9255 Sunset Blvd. (90069)
MOLSON-STANTON ASSOCIATES
  AGENCY, INC. 477-1262
  10889 Wilshire Blvd., Suite 929
  (90024)
MONTAIGNE, EVE, AGENCY   980-3779
  10546 Burbank Blvd., Suite 3,
  N. Hollywood, Calif. (91601)

MONTGOMERY, JO, AGENCY, ARTISTS'
  MANAGER   980-5899
  4429 Carpenter Ave. (91604)
MOORE, LOLA, ARTIST MANAGER
                          276-6097
  9172 Sunset Blvd. (90069)
MORRIS, WILLIAM, AGENCY, INC.
                          274-7451
                          272-4111
  151 El Camino, Beverly Hills,
  Calif. (90212)
  1350 Avenue of the Americas,
  New York, New York (10019)
                     (212) 586-5100
MOSS AGENCY, LTD. 653-2900
  113 N. San Vicente Blvd., Suite 302
  Beverly Hills, Calif. (90211)
MOSS, MARVIN, ARTISTS' MANAGER
                          274-8483
  9200 Sunset Blvd., Suite 601
  (90069)
MULTIMEDIA PRODUCT
  DEVELOPMENT, INC. . . .   276-6246
  170 S. Beverly Dr., Beverly Hills,
  Calif. (90212)
MURPHY, MARY, CONTESSA, JOSEPH,
  AGENCY   985-4241
  10701 Riverside Dr., Toluca Lake,
  Calif. (91602)
NOVEMBER NINTH MANAGEMENT
                          553-4123
  9021 Melrose Ave., Suite 301
  (90069)
OLIVER, MAURINE & ASSOCIATES
                          657-1250
  8746 Sunset Blvd. (90069)
OTIS, DOROTHY DAY, AGENCY
                          461-4911
  6430 Sunset Blvd., Suite 1203
  (90028)
PEARSON, BEN, AGENCY   451-8414
  606 Wilshire Blvd., Suite 614
  (90401)
PICKMAN COMPANY, THE   273-8273
  9025 Wilshire Blvd., Suite 303,
  Beverly Hills, Calif. (90211)

PLESHETTE, LYNN, AGENCY   465-0428
2643 Creston Dr. (90068)

PORTNOY, MILDRED O., AGENCY
                              851-5426
11969 Ventura Blvd. (91604)

PREMIERE ARTISTS & PRODUCTIONS
AGENCY   651-3545
Artists' Manager
6399 Wilshire Blvd., Suite 506
(90048)

PROGRESSIVE ARTISTS AGENCY
                              553-8561
400 S. Beverly Dr., Beverly Hills,
Calif. (90212)

RAISON, ROBERT, ASSSOCIATES
                              274-7217
9575 Lime Orchard Rd., Beverly
Hills, Calif. (90210)

RAPER ENTERPRISES AGENCY
                              461-5033
6311 Yucca (90028)

ROBARDS, BILL, AGENCY   845-8547
4421 Riverside Dr., Toluca Lake,
Calif. (91505)

ROBINSON & ASSOCIATES   275-6114
132 S. Rodeo Dr., Beverly Hills,
Calif. (90212)

ROBINSON-WEINTRAUB &
ASSOCIATES, INC.   653-5802
554 S. San Vicente, Suite 3 (90048)

ROGERS, PHILIP & ASSOC. .   275-5278
9046 Sunset Blvd. (90069)

ROSE, HAROLD, ARTISTS, LTD.
                              652-3961
8530 Wilshire Blvd., Beverly Hills,
Calif. (90211)

ROSEMARY MANAGEMENT   826-3453
11520 San Vicente Blvd., Suite 210
(90049)

RUBEN, SANDY ROTH . . .   271-7209
9418 Wilshire Blvd., Beverly Hills,
Calif. (90212)

RUBY, BETTY, TALENT AGENCY
                              466-6652
1741 Ivar Ave., Suite 119 (90028)

SALKOW, IRVING, AGENCY   276-3141

450 N. Roxbury Dr., Beverly Hills,
Calif. (90210)

SCHALLERT, JOHN W. AGENCY
                              276-2044
450 N. Roxbury Dr., Beverly Hills,
Calif. (90210)

SCHECHTER, IRV, COMPANY   278-8070
404 N. Roxbury Dr., #800,
Beverly Hills, Calif. (90210)

SCHULLER, WILLIAM, AGENCY
                              273-4000
9110 Sunset Blvd. (90069)

SEALOCK, LOIS, AGENCY   473-7130
1609 Westwood Blvd., Suite 204
(90024)

SHAPIRA, DAVID & ASSOCIATES, LTD.
                              278-2742
9171 Wilshire Blvd., Suite 525
Beverly Hills, Calif. (90210)

SHAPIRO-LICHTMAN, ARTISTS'
MANAGER   274-5235
9200 Sunset Blvd.,
Penthouse Suite #7-8 (90069)

SHAW, GLENN, AGENCY. .   851-6262
3330 Barham Blvd., Suite 103
(90068)

SHEPHERD, DON, AGENCY   467-3535
1680 Vine Street, Suite 1105
(90028)

SHERMAN, CHARLIE, AGENCY
                              660-0000
6311 Yucca St. (90028)

SHERRELL, LEW, AGENCY, LTD.
                              461-9955
7060 Hollywood Blvd. (90028)

SIEGEL, JEROME, ASSOCIATES, INC.
                              652-6033
8733 Sunset Blvd., Suite 202
(90069)

SINDELL AGENCY, THE . .   820-2069
11706 Montana Ave. (90049)

SOLOWAY, ARNOLD, ASSOCIATES
                              550-1300
118 S. Beverly Dr., Suite 226,
Beverly Hills, Calif. (90212)

STANLEY, MARGIE, AGENCY   466-3289
1418 N. Highland Ave. (90028)

STIEFEL OFFICE, THE . . . 274-7333
9255 Sunset Blvd., Suite 609
(90069)

STONER, PATRICIA, ARTISTS'
REPRESENTATIVES 980-4449
12069 Ventura Place (91604)

SUGHO, LARRY, AGENCY 657-1450
1017 N. La Cienega Blvd., Suite
303 (90069)

SWANSON, H.N., INC. . . . 652-5385
8523 Sunset Blvd. (90069)

TALENT, INC.. 462-0913
1421 N. McCadden Place (90028)

TANNEN, HERB & ASSOCIATES
466-6191
6640 Sunset Blvd., Suite 203
(90028)

TAYLOR, WILLIAM, AGENCY 550-7271
9000 Sunset Blvd., #805 (90069)

TOBIAS, HERB & ASSOCIATES, INC.
277-6211
1901 Avenue of the Stars, Suite 840
(90067)

TODD, DAVID & CAMARILLO, JAMES
550-1790
9348 Santa Monica Blvd.,
Suite 101,
Beverly Hills, Calif. (90210)

TREJOS & TREJOS LITERARY AGENCY,
ARTISTS' MANAGER . . . 538-2945
18235 Avalon Blvd., Carson, Calif.
(90746)

TRUE AGENCY 874-8474
7513 Fountain (90046)

TWENTIETH CENTURY ARTISTS
990-8580
13273 Ventura Blvd., Suite 211
(91604)

UFLAND AGENCY, INC., THE 273-9441
190 N. Canon Dr., Beverly Hills,
Calif. (90210)

VITT, ANGIE, AGENCY. . . 276-1646
9172 Sunset Blvd. (90069)

WEBB, RUTH 274-4311

9229 Sunset Blvd., Suite 509
(90069)

WEINER, JACK, AGENCY 652-1140
8721 Sunset Blvd. (90069)

WEINTRAUB, MURRY, AGENCY
274-6352
8230 Beverly Blvd., Suite 23
(90048)

WEITZMAN, LEW & ASSOCIATES INC.
278-5562
9171 Wilshire Blvd., Suite 406
Beverly Hills, Calif. (90210)

WITZER, TED, AGENCY . . 278-1926
9441 Wilshire Blvd., Suite 214
Beverly Hills, Calif. (90212)

WORMSER, JACK, AGENCY, INC.
874-3050
1717 N. Highland Ave., Suite 414
(90028)

WOSK, SYLVIA, AGENCY. . 274-8063
439 S. La Cienega Blvd. (90048)

DAN WRIGHT
c/o WRIGHT, ANN ASSOCIATES,
LTD. 655-5040
8422 Melrose Place (90069)
c/o WRIGHT, ANN
REPRESENTATIVES, INC.
136 East 57th Street,
New York, New York (10022)
(212) 832-0110
c/o WRIGHT, ANN
REPRESENTATIVES, INC.
333 Alcazar Ave.
Coral Gables, Fla.
(305) 445-2505

WRITERS & ARTISTS AGENCY
550-8030
9720 Wilshire Blvd., Beverly Hills,
Calif. (90212)
162 W. 56th St., New York, New
York (10019) . . . (212) 246-9029

ZIEGLER, DISKANT & ROTH, INC.
278-0070
9255 Sunset Blvd. (90069)

SCHOOLS AND PUBLICATIONS

In Southern California two of the most highly respected theater arts programs in the country are offered at the University of California at Los Angeles (UCLA), Los Angeles (90024), and the University of Southern California (USC), University Park (90007).

Others in the Los Angeles area are the American Film Institute and the Sherwood Oaks Experimental College.

The American Film Institute is located at 501 Doheny Drive, Beverly Hills, California 90210 (phone: [213] 278–8777). It offers two educational programs: (1) "A one-year structured Curriculum Program open to filmmakers who have obtained some proficiency in their craft. Individuals without experience in film who have experience in related fields—literature, theatre, music, photography and the fine arts—will also be considered." (2) "A Conservatory Program in which emphasis is placed on the work of the individual in his particular field of specialization. Members of this program are selected from among Fellows who have satisfactorily completed the Curriculum Program." The annual tuition for the screenwriting program is $2,600. An endowed library is open to serious movie buffs and aspiring film writers. You may write for a catalog of their screenplay and television script collection.

The Sherwood Oaks Experimental College is located at 6353 Hollywood Boulevard, Hollywood, California 90028 (phone: [213] 462–0669). Instruction in the various subjects is generally offered in six- to eight-week workshop courses. Tuition ranges from $40 to $350 per course. The average is $100 per course.

Other universities and colleges which have exceptionally good theater arts programs include:

University of Chicago, Chicago, Illinois 60637
University of Texas, 200 W. 21st Street, Austin, Texas 78712
Northwestern University, 619 Clark Street, Evanston, Illinois 60201
Columbia University, 630 W. 168th Street, New York, New York 10032

Write to them for their catalogs if you are interested in studying screenwriting on this level. There are many universities and colleges which offer creative writing courses with special instruction in screenwriting. Contact those nearest you.

PUBLICATIONS

The *International Motion Picture Almanac* (published annually by Quigley Publishing Co., 159 W. 53d St., New York, N.Y. 10019) includes film titles, directors, casts, and producers, dating back to the birth of the film industry. It also lists the addresses and phone numbers of all currently active film makers. You can probably find this at your local library. If not, ask them to obtain a copy for you.

Ross Reports lists all current TV shows. Available from Television Index Inc., 150 Fifth Avenue, New York, New York 10011. For New York residents it is $1.55 per issue; for residents of other states, $1.45 per issue.

The *Television Market List,* which is now published in the newsletter of the Writers Guild of America, West, includes names of the various series, brief descriptions of their general concepts, and addresses and phone numbers of the producers and story editors of current shows. Send $2 and a stamped self-addressed envelope to Blanche Baker at Writers Guild of America, West, 8955 Beverly Boulevard, Los Angeles, California 90048.

The *Television Writer's Handbook* by Connie Nash and Virginia Oakey (New York: Harper & Row, 1978) can be found in your local bookstore.

You will want to study as many published screenplays as you can, since there is no better way to learn the nuances of screenwriting. What you have learned in this book you can put to the test in the following ways. Check the essential elements, see how they are developed. Study how narrative and dialog fully develop the plot, provide all necessary exposition, flow upward into crises, and sharply peak to the climax. Watch for the interplay between characters and the taut structure of the scenes. Time the length of the scenes. Whatever you do, don't try to imitate the style of a particular writer, no matter how highly you regard him.

The publishers listed below publish books which contain film scripts. They will supply a list of these books upon request. You can order them direct or through a bookstore.

Appleton-Century-Crofts, 292 Madison Avenue, New York, New
York 10017
Bantam Books, 666 Fifth Avenue, New York, New York 10019
Grove Press, 53 E. 11th Street, New York, New York 10003
Praeger Publications, 111 Fourth Avenue, New York, New York
10003
Signet Books (New American Library), 1301 Avenue of the
Americas, New York, New York 10019
Simon and Schuster (Modern Film Classics), 630 Fifth Avenue,
New York, New York 10020
Universe Books, 381 Park Avenue, New York, New York 10016
Viking Press, 625 Madison Avenue, New York, New York 10022
Yale University Press, 302 Temple Street, New Haven, Connecti-
cut 06511

INTERVIEW—ERIC WEISSMANN
Attorney-at-Law

Eric Weissmann, born in Zurich, Switzerland, was graduated from UCLA College and Law School. He was a member of the legal department of MCA Artists Limited, 1957–60, then became associated with and ultimately a partner in the law firm of Kaplan, Livingston, Goodwin, Berkowitz & Selvin. In 1972–74 Weissmann was a vice-president in charge of business affairs worldwide for Warner Brothers, Inc. He rejoined the Kaplan law firm in 1974, where he represents clients in the entertainment field: writers, directors, film distributors, agents, etc.

Weissmann is a former president of the Los Angeles Copyright Society and has been a lecturer at Harvard University and the Practicing Law Symposium in Washington, D.C. At present he is teaching a course, Legal and Business Aspects of Film, at the Sherwood Oaks Experimental College, Hollywood, California.

Screenwriters should have a general knowledge of the kinds of rights that other people have. By this I mean what is generally called rights of privacy—the rights to write his story about a real event or a real person, to what extent you can use it, to what extent you cannot. If you talk about somebody who is real, to what extent can you fictionalize it, to what extent can you make things up to make it more interesting, to what extent can you lie, to what extent can you trust your sources? How much care do you have to take in making sure that what you write is accurate?

If you use a product in your story you should familiarize yourself with the right that you have to actually depict or use that product. For example, if you use a certain commercially sold product which is, let us say, used to clean windows or to unclog drains and a character forces someone to drink it and kills that person. To what extent can you do that, or do you subject yourself to a claim for libel brought by the product manufacturer? Or to what extent can you show a product in a light for which it was not originally intended? Those are the kinds of things that a writer who writes screenplays or teleplays should have knowledge of and protect himself on.

The next thing screenwriters should consider is the whole area of copyright and public domain. Literary works are subject to protection according to American law, which is the copyright law. Foreign countries have similar laws. Also, countries have treaties with each other whereby they respect each other's laws.

But there is a point when the copyright expires and the work comes into the public domain. Then the question is, can you use that work as a point of departure? For example, *Hamlet* is in the public domain. Can you make a musical called *Hamlet?* Yes, you can. Another example is *Romeo and Juliet.* Can you make a musical about it called *West Side Story* without having to pay anybody for the rights? Yes, you can, because it is in public domain. Then the question is, since *West Side Story* was based on the public domain, can you now rip off *West Side Story* and say it's really *Romeo and Juliet* so you don't have to pay anybody? That answer is no, because while *Romeo and Juliet* is in the public domain the new layer, *West Side Story,* is copyrighted.

Certain events that have actually occurred, historical events, are in the public domain. Anybody can write about the Civil War or Hiroshima or Pearl Harbor. But if somebody else writes about Pearl Harbor, you cannot rip off his writing, because he has put historical events in a certain context and you cannot steal his arrangement of that. For instance, anybody can write a book about Watergate because it was a public event, but you cannot steal *All the President's Men,* because that's not about Watergate only. Two people wrote a book, *All the President's Men,* and used certain characters and certain events and certain relationships. That's their original arrangement of the public domain event. And their original arrangement, as embodied in their original form of literary expression, is entitled to copyright protection.

If an event is used, say, on page 110 of *All the President's Men* but also appeared in seventeen newspaper accounts of the day mentioned, you might be able to use it. It's a thin line you have to draw between what you can do and what you can't do.

How does it become permissible to write about a person? Various ways. One of them is when a person loses his right of privacy. A person is entitled, at least according to American law, to his right of privacy. You are allowed to live your own life as you see fit and be left alone. However, if you voluntarily or involuntarily put yourself in the public view by becoming a movie star or becoming a Nobel Prize winner, by becoming a politician or by murdering somebody, or by being the victim of, or causing or getting involved in, a huge accident—that's what I mean by the voluntary or the involuntary

part—then you are newsworthy and people can write about you in
the newspapers. The courts have extended that and said they can
even do a picture about you, even do a picture about you for profit
—and can even do a picture about you for profit years later. However, there are certain rules governing that picture, and these rules
have been changed a little bit by the court because of the number
of landmark cases. There are certain situations where you can be in
the public view and the passage of time takes you out of the public
view. It depends a little bit on what the subject is. Suppose you were
a famous prostitute and twenty years later when you are leading a
respectable life as a housewife in a little town, they come and make
a picture about you. Maybe you have a lawsuit saying, "I was in the
public eye but that was then, this is now." Furthermore, you might
have a cause for action if the person depicts you inaccurately.

There has been a certain line of cases that says that the public's
"need to know" news is overriding and that the need to gather the
news as quickly as possible makes it difficult for you to be 100
percent accurate. So you can even be inaccurate as long as you're
not recklessly so. As long as you're not maliciously, deliberately,
willfully inaccurate.

There is, however, a distinction between the public's "need to
know" in the case of a public official or "one who has thrust himself
to the forefront of public controversy" and a private individual. The
court has given considerably more leeway to comment and criticism
of the former than of the latter. Private persons do not voluntarily
assume a position in which printed comment on their activities is
expected, and so due care for determining the facts as well as the
avoidance of malice may be required.

One question in considering public domain figures is whether just
the central characters are in public domain or whether the adjunct
characters are too. Again, that's a question of degree. If there is an
accident and you happen to be a bystander, I think that a newspaper
can take a picture of the accident and you can be photographed in
it. If you're the President's secretary, I think that puts you a little
in the limelight too. There is a difference between what I would call
the public limelight and the private limelight. I think that the movie
about Nixon can depict his secretary. But let's not talk about her,
because she became rather famous because of Watergate. Let's consider the clerk who works for her. I think that she can be depicted

a little bit, but I don't think that she can be shown in the bedroom. There are degrees and there are limits to that kind of thing. I think generally you should not. But of course one advantage that you as a writer have is that you don't have to designate that person.

For example, you can do a movie about Nixon and if it's necessary to write about his secretary's clerk, you don't have to identify her. The person only has a right to sue if she can say or prove, "That is me!" If you can say, "Hey, that's not you, you're blond and five foot eight, and this person is a redhead and six foot two. You're a woman and he is a man." So the writer is off the hook.

Concerning copyrights, when a writer is employed by somebody else to write a screenplay (not when he writes a screenplay on his own and sells it himself) it is customary that the employer owns all the rights and owns the copyright as the employer for hire.

The employee has certain minimum protections from the Writers Guild under a doctrine called "Separation of Rights." Basically the Guild says that if the employee creates an original story and screenplay (as distinguished from writing a screenplay based on a story assigned to him by the producer-employer) he has "separation of rights." Or even if the employee is given a story (for example, about the *Titanic*) and he is told "do that" and then with the employer's consent he invents a whole group of new characters and does new things, he has separation of rights in the new material. That gives him certain rights (including the right to additional payment) in case a television series is made from it, or a novel or stage play. Even if he's working on assignment and invents no new characters, he might be able to negotiate for these rights if he is a very powerful writer.

If you write a book or a screenplay and then you sell it, it's a question of the deal that you can make for your material. That's really not a matter of copyright. It's a question of what the deal is. I, as the purchaser, may not get the copyright in the book, but I may get the exclusive motion picture rights in the book and then I can copyright the motion picture and I can write a screenplay. Supposing what I buy is a book, not a screenplay, and then if I cause a screenplay to be written, I own the copyright on the screenplay. The usual deal is that the buyer has the right to show the motion picture, and the author has the right to publish his work. The buyer doesn't have a right to publish the screenplay, because that's competitive to the book. For example, there's a book called *Jaws.* You don't want a screenplay called *Jaws* published, because it will be competitive with the book. That's just a question of bargaining, and that's why you have an agent or lawyer to decide what rights you can keep and what rights you can grant.

The most classic example of where the writer needs protection is if there is a sequel. Say you write a James Bond movie. Does that entitle the purchaser to do seven James Bond movies without paying you anything extra? On the other hand, the purchaser may need protection because he spends a lot of money for the first James Bond picture and he doesn't want another studio to do the next picture. These things generally are worked out as follows: The studio has the right to do sequels and to pay the author additional money for sequels. The author may have the right to write his own sequels, but only after a certain holdback period to give the studio the chance to exploit its original motion picture. Then before the author sells it, he has to go to the studio first to give it a chance to protect its investment and do the next picture. This is called the right of first refusal, and sometimes it's set forth that each time there is a sequel there is the same time period stuff to run all over again. These are the restrictive periods—which mean you can't write a sequel for three years to five years.

The problems seem to occur in the following area: the writer is so thrilled to make a deal that he will sign anything. The motion picture industry used to be rather despotic in dealing with writers. For instance, MGM would not negotiate your contract. You signed their form, take it or leave it. Nobody dared negotiate. Now things are a little bit different. But the problems seem to come mostly because they are overlooked in the original negotiations. Who knew that James Bond would be what it is?

I think the purpose of copyrighting a screenplay would be to establish protection, to establish that you wrote it at a certain time so that if somebody rips it off later he can't claim that he did it. But there are other ways and less complicated ways to establish that than having it copyrighted in Washington, D.C.

One way is to send yourself a registered sealed envelope containing the material and you keep it in a safe unopened, and if there is ever a lawsuit you can prove that on January 9, 1977, this existed and you wrote it.

Another way, even simpler, is for you to register it with the

Writers Guild. You deposit a copy with the Guild and they keep it on file. The cost is minimal for both members and nonmembers.

I really think my advice to a writer, however, would be to have a general familiarization with these areas but not to deal with them himself, because no matter how much he reads he can only get surface information and that won't deal with the real problems that may occur. He should have an attorney or an agent.

Writers also need to know how to bargain on any options taken on their works. An option from the point of view of the seller is less good than a purchase, but you don't always have the bargaining power to demand a purchase. Obviously if I'm Harold Robbins, I don't grant options. But if I'm a young writer, the more usual way to get it off the ground is to grant somebody an option. I had a deal once where I paid $10,000 for thirty days, which is an extreme deal. I represented a talent who felt that he could put a deal together, so he paid $10,000 to have control of the script for thirty days. The writer felt that his talent was pretty hot and if he was going to invest $10,000 of his own money in it, chances were he was going to try real hard. And, indeed, in thirty days he did make a deal, which then allowed for an additional option of eleven months for $40,000.

The reason you grant options is because it is the best you can do and you hope that the other guy is going to put it together for you. Who is the other guy? He can be a studio, or a producer who hopes to attract an important director, or an important male or female star, or whatnot. The hope, of course, is that the option will result in a picture or in a product. The elements to consider when you make an option deal are not only the obvious ones, such as the price that you get or length of time, but also the person with whom you're dealing. If an important studio or an important star or a director takes an option, then your chances are pretty good.

How long is the option period? It depends what the intention of the buyer is and what he needs the option for. He may buy a book or he may buy material which is a screenplay but not quite right. So he'll need to have it rewritten either by you, the writer, or by somebody else more established, more professional, more experienced. That takes time, and when it's rewritten he may need the time to budget it and to try to interest important elements. And elements take time. If you send something to an important star, he's not going to read it that day. You've got to go through his personal managers, his agents, his readers. Or maybe he's busy on the set. He's got a million commitments, and it all takes time. It even takes time for studios, who obviously have the ability to call these stars and their top legal representatives.

I don't think that normally an option for less than a year does the purchaser any good. And normally the purchaser would want at least another year by paying additional money. When I represent a buyer, I insist on one year and I insist on the right to extend it for a second year for an additional payment. I think that a properly negotiated option deal should have everything determined in front. First of all, a buyer doesn't want to spend the option money without knowing what it is going to cost him if he exercises the option. There can be certain sliding scales on the price. For instance, the price can be x dollars if the budget of the picture is a million or less, y dollars if the budget is two million, more dollars if it's three million or more dollars. The idea is that if it is going to be a little picture with a small cast, a no-name cast done on location and privately financed, then they can't afford to pay top price. But if it's going to be a huge production, then they can pay more. There may be an escalation clause in the option agreement that covers this. Sometimes it may even say 5 percent of the budget or 4 percent of the budget. Bear in mind that I'm talking about budget rather than cost.

It would be unfair, in my opinion, for the writer to get more money simply because the picture goes over budget. Budget is what you hope you can make the picture for, and if you are dealing with responsible people the budget will be a responsible budget.

Budgets are prepared by the studio people, or by the production people with the help of the producer. They look at the screenplay and break it down page by page and decide what it will cost. This is a very special science. Then they superimpose upon these very mechanical computations the more subjective computation of how much to budget for certain directors and certain stars. A certain star will need transportation for his wife and his children, and he's going to bring his horse, his motorcycle, or whatever. A certain director will take ten times longer than other directors because he wants to be absolutely super-perfect. There are a lot of variations, and they must all be figured in the budget.

Writers usually want to know if their titles can be protected. Titles, according to American law, are in and of themselves not protectable. However, the courts have realized that there are certain titles which become valuable. They acquire what the court says is secondary meaning. When you think of *Hawaii* you are not thinking just of the island, you are thinking of the best-selling novel by James Michener. So really you shouldn't be able to have another book called *Hawaii,* because people think they are going to reading the Michener book. So the courts have decided to give protection to the owner of the first book titled *Hawaii,* and also to the public so that they don't get ripped off.

Studios want to make sure that titles are protected, at least amongst themselves. So not by law but by contract, they entered into an agreement saying they are going to have a title registration bureau and all of them will become members of it and they agree that if they register a title, no one who belongs to the registration service can rip that title off under certain circumstances. The screenwriter, unless he is also a producer, cannot avail himself of this service. Generally speaking, the title of a screenplay doesn't have much real value, since it has not been published. Titles become valuable, not necessarily because they are so wonderful, but because they become identified with a particular work.

I think that it is very important for writers to familiarize themselves with the Writers Guild agreement, particularly in the area in which they are working.

Publishers generally want to grab as much as they can for themselves, and they also want to control the sale of the film rights. An author should try to keep as much for himself as he can. So my advice is for him to get an agent to control the motion picture sale. And it should be a Hollywood agent. It is better for the agent to be directly responsible to the author, but that's a question of negotiating and bargaining power with the publisher. It depends on what the policy of the publisher is. Some publishers may be more insistent on keeping the screen rights than others. An agent can handle a sale for you for 10 percent. I would hate to pay a publisher more than 10 percent for doing the job less well than an agent does. The publisher does have one advantage in that he has more leverage than a first-time writer and the publisher might be able to get interest from an agent or from a studio that a writer cannot get unless the book is successful. But how many books are terrific, or how many terrific books are successful? So if you are a conservative person and if it's your first or one of your first books, you should make the best deal you can get at the time. That may mean that you sell the motion picture rights first. It may not.

Studios generally insist that the author make warranties that he wrote his screenplay, that he didn't rip it off, and that no rights of third persons are violated. And I think the author probably should warrant that. On the other hand, I don't think the author should warrant against claims. I think the author should only be liable if he breached his warranty. The idea being that the studio or the purchaser is in the business of making motion pictures, whereas the writer is just a guy living in a garret someplace with great inspiration writing things. And I've heard of cases of writers who have been sued and who were liable on their warranties because they warranted against the claims, and they had to defend the lawsuit; they won the lawsuits ultimately, but the expense of defending was more than what they got as the purchase price of their property. The next thing is that some agents try to limit the liability on warranties to the amount you get so they can't take away your house. That's a matter of negotiation. I think that if you ripped off a screenplay, some studios feel that they are damaged, because they have to pay somebody else. They don't care if you do lose your house. And I'm not necessarily unsympathetic to that, because you are a thief.

But it's not always that simple. I can foresee the situation of your not being a thief and of the court still finding against you. Two works may be similar by accident, but you may be unable to convince a jury that you didn't copy.

There is the extreme case of something which was plagiarized, where even the typographical errors were copied. But there are gradations, and I've been involved in situations where very reputable people were sued and it just depends on whom the court believes. Courts are human, too, because they are run by judges and juries and they can make mistakes. So it's an important question; it's an important area. All of these questions underline the fact that it is best to have a lawyer or an agent because they are familiar with these kinds of clauses.

6

Excerpts from Screenplays and Treatment

EXCERPT, *CHINATOWN* BY ROBERT TOWNE

The following pages were excerpted from *Chinatown* to illustrate how expertly a *single scene is constructed through dialog and a minimum of action so that it rises to a sharp and shocking crisis.* Note how the subjects of the shot are identified. Study how the narrative is written into the scene when it follows and precedes dialog, and does not come directly after the subject of the shot.

There is probably no better example of *how exposition is achieved through dialog* than in this scene. Even if you have not seen the movie it becomes clear how dreadful the life of the woman, Evelyn, has been. She is the victim of an incestuous relationship with her father, the mother of a girl who is both daughter and sister, and must wage constant battle to keep from the girl the nature of their relationship. All of this is exposed in dialog, fragmented and frantic, but which has a continuity that keeps the scene moving steadily upward.

224 EXT. BUNGALOW-HOUSE, ADELAIDE DRIVE
     Gittes pulls up in Mulwray's Buick. He hurries to
     the front door, pounds on it.

     The Chinese servant answers the door.
                                           (CONTINUED)

> CHINESE SERVANT
> You wait.

> GITTES
> (short sentence in Chinese)
> You wait.

225   Gittes pushes past him. Evelyn, looking a little worn but glad to see him, hurries to the door. She takes Gittes' arm.

> EVELYN
> How are you? I was calling you.

She looks at him, searching his face.

> GITTES
> - Yeah?

They move into the living room. Gittes is looking around it.

> EVELYN
> Did you get some sleep?

> GITTES
> Sure.

> EVELYN
> Did you have lunch? Kyo will fix you something -

> GITTES
> (abruptly)
> - where's the girl?

> EVELYN
> Upstairs. Why?

> GITTES
> I want to see her.

> EVELYN
> . . . she's having a bath now . . . why do you want to see her?

(CONTINUED)

Gittes continues to look around. He sees
clothes laid out for packing in a bedroom off
the living room.

> GITTES
> Going somewhere?

> EVELYN
> Yes, we've got a 4:30 train to
> catch. Why?

Gittes doesn't answer. He goes to the phone and
dials.

> GITTES
> - J. J. Gittes for Lieutenant
> Escobar . . .

> EVELYN
> What are you doing? What's wrong?
> I told you we've got a 4:30 -

> GITTES
> (cutting her off)
> You're going to miss your train!
> (then, into phone)
> . . . Lou, meet me at 1412 Adelaide
> Drive - it's above Santa Monica
> Canyon . . . yeah, soon as you can.

> EVELYN
> What did you do that for?

> GITTES
> (a moment, then)
> You know any good criminal lawyers?

> EVELYN
> (puzzled)
> - no . . .

> GITTES
> Don't worry - I can recommend a
> couple. They're expensive but you
> can afford it.

(CONTINUED)

                         EVELYN
                    (evenly but with
                    great anger)
              What the hell is this all about?

Gittes looks at her - then takes the
handkerchief out of his breast pocket - unfolds
it on a coffee table, revealing the bifocal
glasses, one lens still intact. Evelyn stares
dumbly at them.

                         GITTES
              I found these in your backyard -
              in your fish pond. They belonged to
              your husband, didn't they? . . . didn't
              they?

                         EVELYN
              I don't know. I mean yes, probably.

                         GITTES
              - yes positively. That's where
              he was drowned . . .

                         EVELYN
              What are you saying?

                         GITTES
              There's no time for you to be
              shocked by the truth, Mrs. Mulwray.
              The coroner's report proves he was
              killed in salt water, just take my
              word for it. Now I want to know
              how it happened and why. I want
              to know before Escobar gets here
              because I want to hang onto my
              license.

                         EVELYN
              - I don't know what you're talking
              about. This is the most insane . . .
              the craziest thing I ever . . .

Gittes has been in a state of near frenzy
himself. He gets up, shakes her.

                                        (CONTINUED)

                        GITTES
          Stop it! - I'll make it easy. -
          You were jealous, you fought, he
          fell, hit his head - it was an
          accident - but his girl is a
          witness. You've had to pay her
          off. You don't have the stomach
          to harm her, but you've got the
          money to shut her up. Yes or no?

                        EVELYN
          . . . no . . .

                        GITTES
          Who is she? and don't give me that
          crap about it being your sister.
          You don't have a sister.

Evelyn is trembling.

                        EVELYN
          I'll tell you the truth . . .

Gittes smiles.

                        GITTES
          That's good. Now what's her name?

                        EVELYN
          - Katherine.

                        GITTES
          Katherine? . . . Katherine who?

                        EVELYN
          she's my daughter.

226   Gittes stares at her. He's been charged with
      anger and when Evelyn says this it explodes. He
      hits her full in the face. Evelyn stares back at
      him. The blow has forced tears from her eyes, but
      she makes no move, not even to defend herself.
                                    (CONTINUED)

                    GITTES
          I said the truth!

                    EVELYN
          she's my sister

Gittes slaps her again.

                    EVELYN
                 (continuing)
          She's my daughter.

Gittes slaps her again.

                    EVELYN
                 (continuing)
          my sister.

He hits her again.

                    EVELYN
                 (continuing)
          My daughter, my sister

He belts her finally, knocking her into a cheap
Chinese vase which shatters and she collapses
on the sofa, sobbing.

                    GITTES
          I said I want the truth.

                    EVELYN
              (almost screaming it)
          She's my sister _and_ my daughter!

                              (CONTINUED)

EXCERPT, *THE SOUND OF MUSIC* BY ERNEST LEHMAN

We include an excerpt from *The Sound of Music* so you can study the eloquence of Ernest Lehman's narrative style, the kind of subjective approach that is possible, and how he uses the camera as a living extension of his unique vision. Notice how the subjects of the shots are identified and how the narrative can be used not only to set the scene but to indicate the desired mood. In these few pages you will find excellent examples of a PANORAMIC (or AERIAL) SHOT, LONG SHOT, REVERSE ANGLE, and TRAVELING SHOT. Note that since *The Sound of Music* is a final shooting script, it does not match exactly the format of the other script examples in this book.

(Lehman)
REVISED - "THE SOUND OF MUSIC" - 12/10/63

"THE SOUND OF MUSIC"

BEFORE MAIN TITLE AND CREDITS

FADE IN:
1 HIGH PANORAMIC SHOT OF THE AUSTRIAN ALPS-LATE
AFTERNOON IN SUMMER

I will not describe the specific locations. I
will tell you the mood, the feeling, the effect
that I would like to see. We are floating in UTTER
SILENCE over a scene of spectacular and unearthly
beauty. As far as the eye can see are majestic
mountain peaks, lush green meadows, deep blue
lakes, the silver ribbon of a winding river.
Isolated locales are selected by the camera and
photographed with such stylized beauty that the
world below, however real, will be seen as a
lovely never-never land where stories such as
ours can happen, and where people sometimes
express their deepest emotions in song. As we
glide in silence over the countryside, we see an
occasional farm, animals grazing in the meadows,
houses nestling in the hills, the steeples of
churches, a castle surrounded by water. And now
something is subtly happening to us as we gaze
down at the enchanted world. FAINT SOUNDS are
beginning to drift up and penetrate our awareness
. . . the tinkle of cowbells . . . the approaching
and receding song of a swiftly passing flock of
birds . . . the call of a goatherd echoing from one
mountain side to another. And with this, we are
aware that the ground seems to be rising. The
treetops are getting closer. Our speed seems to
be increasing. Without knowing it, we have

CONTINUED

1   CONTINUED:

started to approach a mountain. A MUSICAL NOTE is
heard, the first prolonged musical note that
leads to "THE SOUND OF MUSIC." Faster and faster
we skim the treetops. And then suddenly we clear
the trees and reveal:

2   MARIA ON HER MOUNTAIN-TOP

It is a soft and verdant place with a magnificent
panorama of the surrounding countryside. Dressed
as a postulant, but bareheaded, gazing about at
all this breathtaking beauty, is MARIA. As the
musical bridge ends, she whirls into CAMERA in a
CLOSE SHOT and begins to sing "THE SOUND OF
MUSIC," and the CAMERA will drift with her as she
moves about:

                    MARIA
          The hills are alive
          With the sound of music,
          With songs they have sung
          For a thousand years.
          The hills fill my heart
          With the sound of music
          My heart wants to sing
          Every song it hears.

          My heart wants to beat
          Like the wings
          Of the birds that rise
          From the lake to the trees,
          My heart wants to sigh
          Like a chime that flies
          From a church on a breeze,
          To laugh like a brook
          When it trips and falls
          Over stones in its way,
          To sing through the night
          Like a lark who is learning to pray

          I go to the hills
          When my heart is lonely,
          I know I will hear
          What I've heard before.

                              CONTINUED

                            MARIA
                    My heart will be blessed
                    With the sound of music
                    And I'll sing once more.

The MUSIC STOPS. In the silence, DISTANT CHURCH
BELLS ARE HEARD. Maria reacts with alarm. She
grabs her mantilla, which lies nearby, and starts
to run. And as a rousing, full-orchestra
take-away of "THE SOUND OF MUSIC" begins we:
                                        CUT TO:

3   A SERIES OF STYLIZED SHOTS OF THE MAGNIFICENT
    BELL TOWERS OF AUSTRIA'S CHURCHES AND ABBEYS.
    Over these shots, <u>THE MAIN TITLE AND CREDITS
    APPEAR.</u> The bells are heard beneath the music,
    which now includes the strains of other tunes
    . . . "You Are Sixteen" . . . "My Favorite Things"
    . . . "Do Re Mi" . . . "Something Good" . . . "Climb
    Every Mountain." And as we come back to "The Sound
    of Music" for a soft and gentle finish, the MUSIC
    ENDS, THE BELLS FALL SILENT and THE LAST CREDIT
    FADES over:

4   LONG SHOT OF MARIA'S ABBEY - DUSK

    It is a place of stark and simple beauty,
    weathered by the years. Over the shot, a
    SUB-TITLE appears briefly, and fades:

                    "SALZBURG, AUSTRIA,
                    IN THE LAST GOLDEN DAYS
                    OF THE THIRTIES"

    Off-screen, from within the chapel, we HEAR THE
    NUNS' CHOIR CHANTING "DIXIT DOMINUS." It will
    continue during the sequence, until the ending is
    indicated:

                            SOLO
                    Dixit Dominus Domino meo:
                    Sede a dextris meis.

                                    CONTINUED

                    RESPONSE
          Donec ponam inimicos tuos,
          scabellum pedum tuorum.

                    SOLO
          Dominus a dextris tuis,
          confregit in die irae suae reges.

                    RESPONSE
          De torrente in via bibet:
          propterea in exaltabit caput.

                    SOLO
          Gloria Patri, et Filio,
          et Spiritui Sancto.

                    RESPONSE
          Sicut erat in principio,
          et nunc, et semper,
          et in saecula saeculorum.
          Amen.

With the BEGINNING of the chant, we are in the
long shot. At the proper point we:

                              QUICK DISSOLVE TO:

5   HIGH ANGLE – SHOOTING DOWN ON THE CLOISTER OF THE
    ABBEY

    Nuns and novices, singly and in groups, are
    moving quietly and unhurriedly from all
    directions toward the entrance to the chapel
    below us, as the chanting continues.

6   REVERSE ANGLE – THE CLOISTER (FROM GROUND)

    We are closer to the women now as they stream
    across the lawns and gardens toward the chapel
    and the sound of chanting. A novice, carrying
    milk pails on a shoulder yoke, stops to set them
    down before continuing on.

                              CONTINUED

6   CONTINUED:

Another girl leaves her laundry basket behind.
Others have soil-tillers, some have books. The
majestic mountain range beyond the abbey walls,
the loveliness of the cloister, the almost
"choreographed" grace of the women, evoke a
picture of beautiful tranquility here that goes
beyond realism.

7   INT. CHAPEL OF ABBEY

Before the magnificent altar, the MOTHER ABBESS,
SISTER BERTHE, Mistress of Novices, and SISTER
MARGARETTA, Mistress of Postulants, kneel in
prayer. Others come in and take their own places
to pray. In the choir loft, a dozen nuns continue
to chant. On the word "Amen," the chanting
changes to <u>singing:</u>

                    CHOIR
             Rex admirabilis,
             Et triumphator nobilis,
             Dulcedo ineffabilis,
             Totus desiderabilis,
             Totus desiderabilis.

During this, the CAMERA selects visions of
individual beauty and devotion . . . serene
faces, old and young . . . gentle hands clasped in
prayer . . . murmuring lips . . . seen in the light
filtering through stained-glass windows, in the
flickering of altar candles. The SINGING ENDS.
There is an interval of silence. The CHAPEL BELL
SOUNDS ONCE. The Mother Abbess, Sister Berthe and
Sister Margaretta rise and start away. The choir
begins to sing a rather joyous ""ALLELUIA.''

8   TRAVELING SHOT - CORRIDOR OF THE CLOISTER

The Mother Abbess, Sister Berthe and Sister
Margaretta are walking silently along the
corridor that faces the gardens. A rather
worried-looking nun, SISTER BERNICE, hurries
across the courtyard and stops the group.

                                        CONTINUED

                    BERNICE
          Reverend Mother . . .

                  MOTHER ABBESS
          Sister Bernice . . .

                    BERNICE
          I simply <u>cannot</u> find her.

                  MOTHER ABBESS
          Maria?

                    BERNICE
                    (nods)
          She's missing from the Abbey again.

                    BERTHE
                    (tartly)
          Perhaps we should have put a cowbell
          around her neck.

                  MARGARETTA
                    (quickly, protectively)
          Have you tried the barn? You <u>know</u>
          how much she adores the animals.

                    BERNICE
          I've looked everywhere, in all
          the usual places.

                  MOTHER ABBESS
          Sister Bernice, considering that
          it's Maria, I suggest you look
          someplace <u>unusual.</u>

Sister Bernice nods. The Mother Abbess, Sister
Berthe and Sister Margaretta continue on, CAMERA
TRAVELING with them as they talk:

                    BERTHE
                    (caustically - to Mother Abbess)

                    (MORE)

                              CONTINUED

> BERTHE (cont'd)
> Well, Reverend Mother - I hope this
> <u>new</u> infraction helps to clear up
> whatever doubts may have lingered
> in your mind about Maria's future
> here.

> MOTHER ABBESS
> (soothingly)
> I always try to keep faith in my
> doubts, Sister Berthe.

> MARGARETTA
> (to Berthe)
> After all, the wool of a black
> sheep is just as warm.

> BERTHE
> We are not talking about sheep, black
> <u>or</u> white, Sister Margaretta. Of all
> the candidates for the novitiate, I
> would say Maria is the least likely to -

> MOTHER ABBESS
> (interrupting)
> Children . . . children . . .

She is embarrassed, for they have come alongside
the CLOISTER PORCH, and the several nuns who are
grouped there have overheard the rising voices
and slightly heated words. She smiles at the
staring faces.

> MOTHER ABBESS
> It's nothing, my dears. We were
> merely speculating on the quali-
> fications of some of our postulants.
> The Mistress of Novices -
> (indicating Berthe)
> - and the Mistress of Postulants -
> (indicating Margaretta)

> (MORE)

CONTINUED

                    MOTHER ABBESS (cont'd)
          - were trying to <u>help</u> me by
          expressing opposite points of view.
          Sister Catherine, tell me: how do
          you feel about . . . Maria?

                    CATHERINE
          She's a wonderful girl . . .
                    (Margaretta beams)
          Some of the time.
                    (Margaretta stops beaming)

                    MOTHER ABBESS
          Sister Agatha?

                    AGATHA
          It's <u>very</u> easy to like Maria . . .
                    (she frowns)
          Except when it's difficult.

                    MOTHER ABBESS
          And you, Sister Sophia?

                    SOPHIA
          I love her very dearly. But she
          always seems to be in trouble,
          doesn't she?

                    BERTHE
          Exactly what I say!

          They all begin to sing "MARIA."

                    BERTHE
          She climbs a tree and scrapes her knee,
          Her dress has got a tear.

                    SOPHIA
          She waltzes on her way to Mass
          And whistles on the stair.

                                        CONTINUED

EXCERPT, *THE ADVENTURES OF SHERLOCK HOLMES'*
SMARTER BROTHER BY GENE WILDER

In Gene Wilder's *The Adventures of Sherlock Holmes' Smarter Brother* he used the *master scene technique* when describing the incident in which Sigi, the brother, and Orville, his henchman, have just escaped death in a previous scene. They have escaped and find themselves in the midst of a formal ball.

In shot #125 Wilder describes the bare bottoms of both men. However, in the actual shooting of the scene he decided to edit that out so that the audience could participate in the suspense of the moment. We do not know why people seem to be overreacting to the men until Sigi and Orville discover, by looking in a mirror, that their behinds are embarrassingly naked.


```
REVERSE SHOT
Sigi's and Orville's tushies are walking towards
the double doors as the seven Ladies gasp and then
silently faint, one by one.
Sigi and Orville turn around and see SEVEN
UNCONSCIOUS LADIES.

                    SIGI
          Strange.


                    ORVILLE
          I wonder what's got into them?


                    SIGI
          Never mind! Let's get out.


                                        CUT TO:
```

One wall is partially made up of mirrors. A SMALL
ORCHESTRA is PLAYING A MAZURKA. LADIES AND
GENTLEMEN in elegant dress, are dancing and
partaking of refreshments.

Sigi and Orville enter the ballroom thru the
double doors. They are momentarily shocked by
what they see . . . then act out the game and walk
into the room.

They nod greetings to DANCING COUPLES and
PASSERSBY.

Sigi and Orville have become part of a SINGLE LINE
OF MEN facing a SINGLE LINE OF WOMEN. The men
Mazurka to the left as the women Mazurka to the
right. Then, the line of men TURN THEIR BACKS to
the women and Mazurka in the opposite direction.

As they dance SOME COUPLES DROP THEIR MOUTHS in
horror at something they see.

The CAMERA DOLLIES PAST THE FACE OF EACH WOMAN.
They cannot believe what has caught their eyes.

We can now see their naked behinds in the mirror
as they stand surveying the scene.

Some instinct makes them both turn their heads to
the mirror at the same time. Flushed with panic at
the sight of their naked backsides, they both
leap at two nearby ladies and begin dancing
frantically.

SCREAMS from several of the women.

Sigi and Orville clasp hands and dance back to
back towards the front window, smiling. When
they reach the window:

                                        CUT TO:

EXCERPT, *GAME OF PAWNS* BY WILLIAM MacALLISTER

This excerpt shows how *moving shots* (in which the camera moves with the subject) are correctly identified:

                    ZODY
          Or Government support. (The comment
          hits Nichols hard. Zody sees his
          reaction.) Seventy billion, Harry,
          that turns a lot of heads.

Nichols sinks into his seat. Diane hops in back.
Zody puts the jeep into gear. It pulls out into a
pleasant dirt street.

ON THE STREET MOVING

with the jeep as it approaches the closest
intersection. Out of a cross street cruises one
of Phillips' landrovers. The jeep jerks to a
stop.

The landrover stops. In it ride a BRITISH CAPTAIN
and his DRIVER. The officer rises to his feet for
a better look.

Zody jams the jeep into reverse, the vehicle
accelerates backwards.

The landrover takes off in pursuit. The captain
is jerked down to his seat.

THE CAPTAIN

picks up his field telephone.

                    CAPTAIN
          Zebra Delta, Zebra Delta, we have
          Foxtrot. Scramble coordinates . . .

THE JEEP

races backwards, starts to zig-zag violently.

IN THE JEEP MOVING

Diane and Nichols hang on tight. Out the back they
can see two more landrovers turn into the street
behind them.

Zody sees them too. Hitting the brake and almost
stripping gears he jams the jeep into drive and
aims it at the captain's landrover.

NICHOLS AND DIANE

wide-eyed fright.

THE CAPTAIN AND HIS DRIVER

panic.

THE LANDROVER

swerves out of the way, scrapes by the jeep.

IN THE JEEP - MOVING

                    ZODY
          Chicken bastards!

THE LANDROVER

runs into the curve, bounces out of control,
slams into the porch of a nearby house.

IN THE JEEP - MOVING

Zody's victory is short-lived. A fourth and
fifth landrover turn into the street ahead of
them. Zody brakes abruptly.

                    NICHOLS
          (shouting, as if the momentary
          inertia could be shocked into
          action)
     MOVE! DAMN IT! HANG A "U"!

THE JEEP

shoots off the street; bounces over curb, lawns,
gardens. It does a 180 turn.

The following excerpt from MacAllister's *Game of Pawns*
illustrates how the subject of the shot, though moving, is *not necessarily a moving shot.*

EXT. ON THE ROOF OF THE ADJOINING HOUSE

Nichols dives out a window. He rolls across the
roof. The Beard is at the window. He fires off a
pair of shots. Nichols is over the edge. The
bullets ricochet off an empty roof.

ALLEY

Nichols hits the ground running. He scrambles
downhill.

BACK UP AT THE HOUSE

Dollface and the lithe Panga-Man scramble out the
front door.

ON THE ROOF OF THE ADJOINING HOUSE

the Beard is out the window and giving chase
across the roof.

ON THE PATH - DOLLFACE

shouts at the Panga-Man. The lithe
machete-wielding man runs headlong down the
hill. Dollface leaps up on the roof of the
adjoining house. He drums across it.

THE BEARD

pistol in hand, crouches on the edge of the roof
and scans the alley below for Nichols. Dollface
runs past him and off the roof.

DOWN IN THE ALLEY

Dollface lands like a cat. He shouts up at the
Beard to follow and then dashes down the alley
after Nichols. The Beard lands in the alley, then
scrambles off between the houses.

EXCERPT, TREATMENT FOR *KATIE'S LADIES* BY CONSTANCE NASH

The following three pages from *Katie's Ladies,* (screenplay currently under option) will show you how the first page of a treatment is written, how the format is set up, what it must include (scene and character descriptions, action, and some dialog), and the tempo it sets for the ensuing narration. From these pages the reader will know what kind of picture it will be—a farce set in the American West in the 1890s. The complete treatment is 32 pages long; these pages represent about the first fifteen minutes of film.

"KATIE'S LADIES"
Written by
Constance Nash
7/25/75

SETTING

The mountainous territory around Virginia City, Nevada, late 1800's during the silver mining era.

ACT ONE

Dust swirls are churning around a horse-drawn carriage as it moves toward us on the main street of Carson City.

KATIE, a Madame and a fiery-tempered redhead, is driving the carriage hell-bent-for-leather toward the COURT HOUSE. She stops, jumps from the rig, motions to a by-stander to water her sweating horse and storms into the court—in what seems to be one continuous movement.

We see the JUDGE, a bearded lustful-looking man who, upon catching sight of Katie, drops the gavel and the sentencing simultaneously. "Guilty—one year—all five of 'em."

The packed courtroom resounds with a collective moan of obvious disappointment as Katie barrels down the aisle, hands on hips, face set, toward the judge. He gathers up his robe and gavel and hightails it to his chambers but not soon enough to escape Katie who is right on his heels.

"Why, Katie, my sweet, what brings you thundering into the county seat on a hot day like this?"

"You know damn well. You're actin' mighty peculiar lately—now you'll just have to pardon them."

"Calm yourself, lass. I'm appointed to *uphold* the law. Now what kind of judge would I be if I pardoned their crime and let 'em go?"

"The same kind you've always been—crooked."

"Katie, lass. (He sidles over to her with a familiarity we'll become accustomed to.) Why don't you lay down, rest yourself after the long ride . . ."

"Oh, no you don't. I'm not here to be sweet-talked out of my senses. You git off that dead ass of yours and pardon them before we lose our money to the first bunch of dirty robbers who hear about your stupidity." She walks over and pours herself a drink as the judge tries to figure his way around her anger toward his own objective, the appeasement of his overactive libido.

Whispering behind her ear, he says, "My ass is far from dead . . ."

She cuts him off. "Well, you're goin' to be wishin' it was!" She slugs down the whiskey and storms out. He calls out to her to try to understand; he is planning on running for the U.S. Senate.

The problem Virginia City faces is this: the town has enjoyed a perverse compromise with the local gang of train robbers who reside in the town, do their dirty deeds elsewhere, and protect the local banks, saloons and bordellos from marauding bands.

The sheriff exists in name only.

DISSOLVE to Virginia City and Katie's bordello. Katie has just walked in. Several girls in scanty attire are draped about the rococo parlor waiting for her. Business is slow. The PIANO PLAYER is a droll, comedic type who is busy plunking out tunes.

Nearby is a handsome bar and stage. RUBY, a bit of a comic, is performing for nobody on stage. She can't sing worth a damn.

A door above the balcony opens and we see COOKIE, a two-hundred-pound honey who likes to bake and have little tea parties for her guests. Walking out behind her is the SHERIFF, a gentle, passive man with a build like a pipe cleaner. He is buttoning up.

Katie fills the girls in on the news and they are discussing the pros and cons of drawing their respective savings out of the local wealthy bank before anybody comes to town with larcenous ideas.

Suddenly we hear exuberant YELPING and GUNFIRE out on the main street. BLOSSOM, a shapely, buxom, never-bright girl, runs to the lace-curtained window to see what the activity is all about.

Katie is right on her heels. The town's fear has become an immediate reality. A notorious band of "bad guys" is riding up and down the main street, playfully scaring the populace which is now cowering behind windows, doors and poles.

The PATCH GANG is led by PATCH, as engaging an outlaw as you'd ever want to see. He is waving and smiling broadly like a warrior home from the wars.

Katie tells Blossom to bolt the door. She must think. The bandits stand outside and call to the girls. Blossom loves it and giggles and waves from the window. Ruby gets back on the stage, readying for a new audience. Cookie runs to the kitchen to stave off nervousness, while the Piano Player changes his tune to a CHURCH HYMN.

Patch shoots the lock out and in waltz the gang. Katie marches up to Patch and standing nose to nose tells him the new house rules. Bath Before Business. They refuse.

Cut to the main bank. We see the nervous officials huddled in a meeting. Standing outside the bank observing the action down the street is MISS HORTENSE, a prim spinster lady and bank employee. She isn't as old or as starched as we might at first think.

Cut to the bordello. The gang are grumbling about the house rules for newcomers—until they catch sight of Blossom ambling down the stairs in a cinched French corset, black stockings, garters and her ample bosom flopping about with each step. She is carrying a dozen towels.

As soon as they realize what is happening in the bathhouse they drop their trousers in unison. All we see is a profusion of elbows and asses as they stumble over their trousers toward the huge wooden tub. INTO VIEW in the steaming room is Ruby. She is coquettishly gesturing to them.

While the gang are being bathed Katie sends all their clothing to the Chinese laundry across the back alley. Under no circumstances are the clothes to be dried.

Patch gets suspicious when all of them begin to look like prunes. He calls for clothes. Realizing they've been duped he steps from the tub, straps on his holster, and walks out to the parlor, wet and stark naked. He calmly heads for the laundry.

Index

actors, scripts sent to, 88
acts, divisions of script, 2–3, 20–21
*Adventures of Sherlock Holmes'
  Smarter Brother, The,* Wilder,
  137–138
agencies, listed, 103–109
agents, literary, 54, 75–79, 85–89, 120
American Graffiti, 72, 78–79
audio instructions, 36–37

Bergman, Ingmar, 37
Brown, Charlotte, 88
budgets of films, 61–62, 119

camera angle descriptions, 30–31
characterization, 4–7; by dialog, 7–10
characters, emphasis on, 1, 60–61;
  minor, 7
Chayefsky, Paddy, *Marty,* 3
Chinatown, Towne, 20, 23–25, 61,
  122–127
clichés, 16, 83
climax as element of screenplay, 2, 3
code ratings of films, 73–74
comedy, difficulty of, 69–70
conflict as element of screenplay, 2
consistency: of characters, 5; of
  dialog, 13–15

contracts, 54–56, 78, 89; Writers
  Guild, 99–103
contrast, in characterization, 5–6
Coppola, Francis Ford, *The
  Godfather,* 7–8, 13–14, 26–27, 62
copyrights, 89, 113–114, 116–117
costume, in character exposition, 6
credibility, 40–41
crisis as element of screenplay, 2, 122

deals, *see* contracts
dialog: consistency of, 13–15;
  naturalness of, 11–12; tempo of, 12;
  uses of, 7–11, 122
directors, 64–68, 77, 83, 87–88;
  relations with writers, 56, 66–69,
  81–82
distribution of films, 71–72

Elder, Lonne, III, *Sounder,* 5, 10–11,
  14–15
emotional involvement in screenplay,
  ix-x, 37, 39
environment, influence on characters,
  6
Evans, Robert, interview with, 58–63
exposition, 38–39, 54; of characters, 6;
  through dialog, 38–39, 122

fees, Writers Guild scales, 100–101
financing of films, 61–62, 71–74
Ford, Tony, 86
format: of script, 43–49; for television, 47–48; of treatment, 142–145
frame, defined, 22, 28

Game of Pawns, MacAllister, 139–141
Godfather, The, Coppola and Puzo, 7–8, 13–14, 26–27, 62

imitation, 15

Katie's Ladies, Nash, 142–145

legal advice, 113–121
Lehman, Ernest: interview with, 51–57; The Sound of Music, 128–136

MacAllister, William, Game of Pawns, 139–141
Maggie Walker, Ziegler and Oakey, 8–10
Mann, Delbert, interview with, 64–70
Manuscript Registration Service, 91–93
marketing: of scripts, 62–63, 78, 87–88; of talent, 85–89
Marty, Chayefsky, 3
master scene style of screenplay, 22, 26–27, 137–138
material, choice of, 51
monologs, 12
motivation of characters, 5
moving shots, examples, 35–36, 139–141
musical scores, 57

narrative, uses of, 23–25, 26, 45, 46, 122–128
Nash, Constance, Katie's Ladies, 142–145; Television Writer's Handbook, 48, 86

Oakey, Virginia, Maggie Walker, 8–10; Television Writer's Handbook, 48, 86
options, 89, 118–119
outline, 19; title page of, 46–47

plagiarism, 74, 121
privacy, rights of, 113, 114–115
producers, 58–59, 64–65, 72–73, 82–83
public domain, 114–116
publications for screenwriters, 111–112
publishers and film rights, 120–121
Puzo, Mario, The Godfather, 7–8, 13–14, 26–27, 62

registration of material, 91–93, 117–118
rewriting, 41–42, importance of, 17, 57
rights: of ownership, 116–117; of privacy, 113, 114–115
Rosenfelt, Frank, interview with, 71–74
rough draft of screenplay, 37–41

scenes, to write, 20, 27
schools of screenwriting, 110–111
scripts: division into acts, 2–3, 20–21; format, 43–49; handling of by studio, 62–63; importance to film, 59–60; length of, 21, 68; number of copies, 48–49; sources of, 111–112; on speculation, 88–89; unsolicited, 74
Separation of Rights, doctrine of, 116
sequels, 117
shooting script, format of, 128–136
shot-by-shot style of screenplay, 22–26, 122–127, 128–136
shots, defined, 22, 28, 30–36
situation as element of screenplay, 1, 2
Sound of Music, The, Lehman, 128–136
Sounder, Elder, 5, 10–11, 14–15
special effects shots, 31–33
Spelling, Aaron, 86
stereotypes, 4
style, 15–17
subject-in-motion shots, 35–36, 128
symbolism, 16
synopsis, 19, 20, 74

techniques of writing, 52–54, 80–84
television: financing of, 74;

television *(cont'd)*
  script formats, 47–48
Television Writer's Handbook, Nash
  and Oakey, 48, 86, 111
tempo: of dialog, 12; of script, 12
terminology of screenplays, 27–37
title page formats, 43–44, 46–47
titles, 51–52; protection of, 119–120
Towne, Robert, *Chinatown,* 20,
  23–25, 61, 122–127
transitional instructions, 34–35
treatments, 4, 18–19, 46–47, 142–145
typewriter settings for scripts, 44–46

unsolicited scripts, 74

vocabulary, screenwriter's, 27–37

warranties, 121
Weissmann, Eric, interview with,
  113–121

Wilder, Gene: interview with, 80–84;
  *The Adventures of Sherlock Holmes'
  Smarter Brother,* 137–138
women, roles for, 60–61
writer: importance of to film, 59–60;
  relations to agent, 75–76, 77–78;
  relations to director, 56, 66–69,
  81–82
Writers Guild of America, West,
  90–103; functions and services,
  91–95; Guild Shop information,
  98–99; membership, 90–91, 95–98
writers representatives, *see* agencies
writing techniques, 52–54, 80–82,
  83–84

Ziegler, Isabelle, *Maggie Walker,*
  8–10
Zimring, Michael, interview with,
  75–79